COUNTING THE DANCE STEPS

RETHINKING HOW WE MEASURE AND CHANGE ORGANISATIONAL
CULTURES FOR THE GOOD OF ALL

ANDREW COCKS

Copyright © Andrew Cocks, 2022

All rights reserved.

No part of this book may be reproduced, stored in or introduced into a retrieval system, or transmitted in any form or used in any manner (electronic, mechanical, recording or otherwise) without written permission of the copyright owner except for the use of quotations in a book review. For more information, address: andrew@andrewcocks.info

First paperback edition April 2022

Grateful acknowledgement to the good people from Tivian for all their help and support in conducting much of the original research cited in this book. Thank you also to Professor Edgar Schein for his helpful input into, and kind endorsement for Counting the Dance Steps.

ISBN 978-1-7396576-0-4 (paperback)

ISBN 978-1-7396576-1-1 (ebook)

IBSN 978-1-7396576-2-8 (hardback)

For Rachel, Eleanor and Gabriel....

and Ned

CONTENTS

PREFACE 7
INTRODUCTION 12
GOOSE OR STARLING? 24
MIMI'S STORY 55
IT'S QUIET….TOO QUIET 58
THERE'S A WOLF IN MY KITCHEN 84
EVERYBODY DANCE! 88
WELCOME TO THE TERMITE MOUND 107
TURNING TADPOLES INTO FROGS 110
TRUST EVERYONE, AND TRUST NO ONE 122
WHEN FOREHEAD MEETS WALL 130
I SEEM TO HAVE LEFT MY LEG ON THE TRAIN! 135
TWO STORIES, ONE INCONSEQUENTIAL 152
COUNTING THE DANCE STEPS 155
MIMI'S STORY CONTINUED 181
UNCOVERING CORE ASSUMPTIONS 183
PUTTING THE RIGHT MUSIC ON 188
THE FUTURE OF CULTURAL ASSESSMENT & MANAGEMENT 204
CONCLUSIONS 214

COUNTING THE DANCE STEPS

PREFACE

I had only been at the bank for a few months when I was unexpectedly called into a meeting. Sitting in the room were a number of senior members of the Risk and HR functions. It soon became clear that HSBC had been accused of providing money-laundering services to the tune of many hundreds of millions of dollars to Mexican and Colombian drug cartels in the late noughties, and the bank was to conduct an internal investigation into the causes of this. This was not a small matter as the US authorities had threatened to revoke the bank's charter to operate in the United States in response. I had been summoned to the meeting as I was to lead a part of the investigation process, by conducting research into the precursors of this failure. This was to be done through an assessment of Mexican employees, to gauge the extent to which they understood the company's internal rules and procedures. This was telling. There was clearly an assumption that the only possible explanation for this kind of lapse was that people were unaware of what was expected of them. It was not possible that anyone could conceivably allow this to happen if they were fully aware of the rules and regulations governing their behaviour, could it?

PREFACE

As part of the ensuing investigation, interviews were conducted with HSBC Mexico leadership and a sample of employees, along with the administration of an online assessment of all employees. Early in the process, it became very clear that the expectations around standards of behaviour between the leadership at the centre and the staff across the branch network had been stretched so thin that they had reached breaking point. This meant that the different groups of employees were playing by completely different rules and that neither party was aware of the threat the bank was being placed under. It also became very clear that while understandably somewhat defensive, the overriding reaction of those responsible for compliance and risk management to the events was one of utter bewilderment. How could such vast amounts of dirty money be processed right under their noses without anyone with responsibility for oversight being aware of what was happening? How could both the internal checks and balances as well as those of external regulators fail so spectacularly?

In response to the subsequent threat from US authorities, HSBC Holdings agreed to pay a $1.9 billion fine in recognition of its failures. HSBC were not alone, ING, Barclays, and Credit Suisse also had to pay fines for similar separate transgressions at around the same time. The resulting investigations into all these failures provide a glimpse of a shadowy world beyond the shiny glass towers and sharp suits where the many can do heinous things, while convincing themselves and everyone else that all is well. A world where the few who do speak up are ignored until they just don't bother any more, where leadership prefers to believe the good news and doesn't look for the bad. Where intelligent, honourable individuals can come together and collectively act in ways that were very far from intelligent and honourable. Where people can convince themselves that black is white, and that grey doesn't even exist. A world where anyone can persist in the belief that everything is OK until shockingly and unexpectedly, it very obviously isn't.

COUNTING THE DANCE STEPS

Despite the extraordinary context under which the research programme I helped to implement was conducted, the results hinted at nothing unusual or untoward. Employees demonstrated a reasonably high level of understanding of risk management processes and generally reported that all was well. The reason for this apparent paradox was clear from early on, and ultimately came as no surprise. We were looking in the wrong places and asking the wrong questions. But one question remained, how could we possibly have got beneath the veneer of integrity and propriety to uncover the truth behind such transgressions, when even those closest to them are unable or unwilling to recognise that anything was wrong, until the impact of their actions was rubbed in their faces? Under these circumstances, in future how could we possibly ever get to a place where we can anticipate and prevent something like this from happening again?

Some years later after having left HSBC and starting my own consulting business, Conflux, I was listening to the BBC radio news as I do most mornings, when something struck me. There were various news stories reported, which focused on the latest disasters, wrongdoings and scandals. That day it was NHS Mid Staffs, BBC and Jimmy Savile and LIBOR. It appeared that across these diverse issues in very different institutions there was a common contributory cause for failure, organisational culture. It seemed that culture was, at least in part, to blame for all these scandals. It was assumed that this thing called culture had the power to wreak untold havoc, destroy lives and reputations and even threaten to bring down the biggest institutions and corporations. It was what we had begun to touch upon in our investigations at HSBC, but ultimately what had eluded us. Once I became attuned to this emerging narrative, in almost every news bulletin I subsequently listened to, there continued to be a steady stream of ethical or moral failures that were squarely blamed on organisational culture. What was notably absent in all this discourse was any real clarity about what culture was, how it worked, or what to do about it.

PREFACE

For the previous 15 years I had been working with and for large organisations conducting research into the experiences and opinions of their employees. This had concentrated on how employee experience impacted on business outcomes such as turnover, performance, efficiency, and profitability. As someone focused on research, gathering and interpreting empirical evidence to reach conclusions, it seemed to me that throughout this emerging media narrative about organisational culture, people were being very quick to talk in such absolutist terms about something so poorly defined. But I was also guilty. Much of the work I had done up to that point had had no explicit link to culture, yet I had myself on many occasions talked about culture in a vague and lazy way when dealing with colleagues and clients. I had led culture audits intended to investigate the causes of lapses in compliance and risk-management processes in public sector and financial institutions. I had designed and managed large surveys of hundreds of thousands of employees branded as culture surveys. In truth these were not distinct from any other kind of employee surveys that have become almost ubiquitous over the last 20 years, and I now know certainly didn't do more than scratch the surface of culture. In my further education and recent work, I had acquired a passing familiarity with academic definitions and models of culture as well as some of the most common cultural assessment tools. I was however, still a very long way from being able to talk with any authority on the subject. How could someone like me, working in such a closely related area, be so ill-informed about something so fundamental and powerful? Very early on in my subsequent inquiry I was to learn that I was far from alone. Many of my fellow management consultants were also prone to speak with false authority on the subject of culture. We could do this because we were able to hide behind the convenient line that there is something inherently nebulous and unmeasurable about it.

Since that day I have both personally and professionally become fascinated by organisational culture, how it works and how we can change it. This book is the result of my subsequent professional experience, research and musings on the subject. What prompted me to embark on this endeavour was my growing belief that much of what was said about organisational culture is either lazy and questionable, wilfully designed to obfuscate and confuse, or just downright false. In this book I have attempted to challenge the current orthodoxy and provide some suggestions for new and potentially more productive ways of conceptualising, measuring and changing culture. Hopefully it will contribute to a more thoughtful and less dogmatic conversation around how we manage organisational culture, which is after all far too important and consequential to continue getting so catastrophically wrong.

COUNTING THE DANCE STEPS

INTRODUCTION

Most of the time our business leaders like to give the impression they are in control. They analyse, strategise, pull the levers of reward and sanction and tinker with structures, policies and processes. They issue bold statements about core values and commitment to their customers, employees, social and environmental responsibility and they tell themselves that they mean every word. Everyone else sees their actions, hears the commitments and increasingly, they don't believe any of it.

Our captains of industry may have their hands on the tiller, but the ship largely still goes where the currents take it. Their continued inability to understand culture and how it works means that in truth, they are very far from in control. The cultures of large organisations, by their very nature cannot be directed from on high by their senior leadership. They are not governed by rational, formal, structures and procedures which can be planned and controlled through policy and strategy. They are largely self-organising, evolving and changing without regard for the aspirations of leadership, driven by implicit beliefs and assumptions that determine how the people within them behave. If we continue in our failure to understand how these forces operate and to take conscious steps to influence them,

INTRODUCTION

things will inevitably deviate from the charted course. Bad and unintended things will happen as to err is fundamentally human. When things do go wrong, cynicism is fuelled because the assurances leaders give about their values and goals are exposed as being largely hollow. They are hollow because the lack of control means there is often a gulf between what they say they stand for and the actions and decisions taken by themselves and others within their organisations.

When behaviours clearly run counter to espoused values, our leaders are presented with a challenge. If they were truly in control, as they like to believe they are, then they should be held to account. Historically, many leaders have been quick to circle the wagons and deny any wrongdoing. More recently, they have been quick to point out in their defence that these things happen without their consent or even their knowledge, with rogue perpetrators operating outside the normal parameters of acceptable behaviour. After all, when did a leader ever exhort their employees to take unacceptable risks, unfairly exploit customers or discriminate against female or minority group employees? Hopefully never, and yet these things all too frequently keep happening.

The recent media narrative has greatly increased the likelihood of this kind this response being deployed. In an attempt to explain why bad things continue to occur, and define where the lines of responsibility lie, when things go wrong we have built a defence that this is caused by something powerful, complex, and illusive, and therefore beyond anyone's ability to directly control. We increasingly hear this mysterious force referred to as 'culture' which we are told operates at the fuzzy edges where priorities conflict, accountabilities are blurred, and spheres of influence are ill-defined. This means that almost anyone can inflict financial or reputational damage by simply doing the wrong thing without the knowledge of leadership or supervisory functions. This narrative has been enthusiastically adopted as it has served our business leaders, the media, regulators and management consultancies very well over recent years. How can we expect our leadership to effectively grapple with something so complex and illusive that lurks in the shadows, beyond anyone's capacity to see or quantify?

Our continued inability to consistently define, understand, measure, and manage organisational culture is shameful. The self-serving and convenient lies and half-truths we are constantly peddled regarding the nature of culture are a huge part of the problem. Foremost amongst these is the assertion that culture is complex and intangible, beyond anyone's ability to directly measure or control. We are in fact perfectly capable of understanding and getting a grip on measuring organisational culture, but to do so we first need to strip away all the misleading received wisdom and take a fresh perspective on how culture works. Until we do all the assurances given by our business leaders regarding commitment to ethical practice, society, customers, and the environment will remain hollow and meaningless.

Like never before, leaders of organisations of all kinds are being forced to re-examine their values, purpose, and the role they play in society. This is because public trust in institutions is lower than it's ever been and seemingly in freefall. We are at a turning point. Any mismatch between what these institutions purport to value and stand for and their actions would until recently have been seized upon as an example of a lack of honesty or integrity. There would be consequences. Increasingly these mismatches are being greeted with a collective shrug; what else can we expect from big business, political parties or public institutions? This means that integrity is losing its currency and when this happens, organisations no longer come under scrutiny and offenders will be less and less likely to ever be held to account. It's time for these organisations to seize the initiative and take steps to reverse this decline in trust before it erodes altogether. This can only be done if they understand and take steps to influence the forces that are really driving the behaviours of the individuals and groups that make them up. So why

INTRODUCTION

don't we do it? A large part of the reason has to be because we think we know how.

> *'The trouble with culture is everyone blames it when things go wrong but no-one really knows what it is or how to change it.'*
>
> Professor Jon Glasby quoted from the Francis Report

This is a quote used in the most comprehensive investigation into one of the most shocking organisational cultural failures of recent times. The Francis Report was commissioned by the UK government to investigate this scandal, and it catalogued a litany of failures in patient care in the Mid Staffordshire NHS Trust which resulted in immense unnecessary suffering and death. The full report runs to hundreds of pages and took over two years to produce. The inquiry was set up in November 2010 to examine the failure of regulators to spot poor standards of care within the Trust's hospitals. These failings had profound consequences, with 500 more deaths recorded across the Trust than would normally have been expected between 2005-6 and 2007-8.

Over many years, stories of patient mistreatment at Stafford Hospital had become legion with patients and their families reporting unsanitary conditions on the wards, poor standards of patient care and medical attention being withheld for unacceptably long periods of time. Patients were left lying on soiled bed sheets and medically unqualified staff were left to triage patients in the Accident and Emergency Department. A report from the Healthcare Commission published in March 2009 described the standards of care at Mid Staffordshire as "appalling." The independent inquiry, chaired by Robert Francis, reported in 2010 that failures in patient safety and care were caused by a culture that tolerated inadequate training of staff and staff shortages, and overemphasised government targets. In November 2010 the full public inquiry began, again chaired by Francis. The word 'culture' is used no fewer than 486 times in the resulting Francis Report. Culture is indeed blamed for many of the organisational failings detailed in the report and yet only a portion of a single page is dedicated to defining what culture is and how it works, culminating in the above quote. How can we be so quick to put our hands up in surrender?

In the absence of a thorough understanding of culture and how it works, it is both lazy and convenient to blame systematic problems on culture. Accountability is obscured if we accept that this thing called culture operates purely subliminally, where it can exert its effects unseen in an insidious and often malign way, beyond the means of anyone to directly influence. This way individual responsibility is diluted in a generalised sense and everyone and no one is implicated. There seems to be some kind of truce between the media and the leaders of our institutions when things go wrong. They collude to blame culture as it serves both parties pretty well under the circumstances. It provides the accuser a means of giving the appearance of holding the perpetrators to account while not taking the risk of directly accusing them of culpability. It avoids the risk of exposing themselves to accusations about their obvious inability to manage their own cultures. It also provides the accused the opportunity to blame something that they claim to be neither consciously aware of, nor within their sphere of control.

Daniel Morgan was a private investigator. In 1987 he was found with an axe in his head in a South London pub car park. His murder was investigated by the Metropolitan Police no fewer than 4 times, despite which, the crime remains unsolved to this day, and nobody has ever been charged or convicted. In 2021, an independent review into the handling of the investigation of Morgan's murder was published. It found that the Metropolitan Police had "a culture of institutional corruption" in that it had obstructed the inquiry by repeatedly concealing or denying its failings in the case. In response to this, the Constabulary's defence in the media was to challenge the definition of the word 'corruption'. Noticeably they didn't challenge the assertion that it was the force's culture that was at fault. Instead, they chose to question the meaning of a word which is infinitely clearer

INTRODUCTION

in its definition. It seemed that the word 'culture' was acceptable to deploy as this rather neatly distanced the issue from the direct responsibility of Police leadership or any individual officers. Contrast this with the Met's reaction to the publication of the Macpherson report into their failings in relation to the investigation into the murder of black teenager Stephen Lawrence in 1998, in which the force was described as 'institutionally racist'. While they clearly did not relish being labelled 'racist', it was the word institutionally that the Met took a particular exception to. Given that the phrase '*institutionally racist*' would almost certainly now be supplanted with the phrase *'a culture of racism'*, the difference between these two responses is telling. It appears that the Metropolitan Police have, since Macpherson, learned the benefits of hiding behind the powerful responsibility diffuser that the culture has come to be.

There are a number of common assertions about organisational culture that have become so ubiquitous they are almost universally accepted seemingly without question. The view that culture is so complex and illusive that it can only be understood and addressed by expert practitioners and therefore very difficult to measure and quantify, has been propagated by academics applying advanced psychological models and consultants selling expensive assessment and management services. It has fuelled the false belief that responsibility for culture lies with the privileged few who have the knowledge and expertise to grapple with it. This has meant that the normal default setting for senior leadership who are charged with addressing cultural issues is to delegate responsibility for managing culture to specialists within an HR function or to seek help from external consultants. Even with this 'expert' guidance, the management consultancy firm McKinsey famously estimated that 70% of culture change programmes fail. Quite an admission from one of the firms claiming to specialise in this area. Culture change is universally characterised as being difficult and time consuming, requiring the allocation of enormous resources from across a range of leadership and functional groups. McKinsey and many others also repeatedly stress that you cannot simply copy the culture of a successful organisation, because every culture is unique and there is no one size fits all solution. None of these common assumptions is true.

Let's summarise the current prevailing narrative.

Your culture can be your competitive advantage. Get it right and there are untold benefits. Get it wrong and it could destroy you. It is however almost unfathomably complex with so many different interacting elements to culture that we need deploy complex academic models if we are to even attempt to understand it. This means that culture change lies within the remit of academics and expensive specialist consultants. Change must be sponsored by senior leadership who will ultimately have to carry the can when things go wrong, which is likely to be often as we have a historical track record of abject failure in culture change. This is because culture is next to impossible to measure, meaning you cannot diagnose what needs to be done or quantify any change. We cannot consistently define what a 'good' culture looks like and while strategy and business practises can be copied, culture cannot. This means you're on your own and there are no best practises that you can draw on to help you. Even if you tried to understand and change culture the resources and time required to implement a successful change programme will be huge, and the chances of success are slim.

Is it any wonder there is a reluctance to tackle culture head on? If we are to accept this narrative, we will forever more be bemoaning an endless litany of disasters and corporate scandals. Most importantly we will be unable to respond to the challenges that we face as a society from social and racial injustice and environmental degradation.

We appear to be stuck in a rigid mindset which says the only way we can conceptualise and influence culture is at the macro organisational level, by

INTRODUCTION

attempting to think about it in its entirety. This effectively means that, to even attempt to understand it, we have to use an academic lens as culture assessment and change lies beyond the capabilities of most lay people to understand. Hopefully in this book, I can show you that nothing could be further from the truth. Culture is about collective behaviour. There is nothing intangible about behaviours and the forces that shape them can be easily exposed. The McKinsey statistic about the lack of success does show that historically we have not made life easy for ourselves. Why is this? First, we have not paid enough attention to the mechanism by which culture works, how it is formed and why it can be so resistant to change. Without an understanding of this mechanism, we simply cannot permanently change culture or identify the barriers to doing so. While we need a simple lens through which culture can be measured and changed, we continue to either use assessment tools like employee surveys, that are not fit for purpose, or we use tools based on complex, academic models that very few understand. You may be familiar with these. They are usually easy to spot as they tend to look like multicoloured dartboards or spiders' webs with lots of words around the outside representing numerous different indices. They are most often developed by Occupational Psychologists, requiring specialist training to administer and interpret. What they don't do is give time-poor managers and staff what they really need, a clear view of how they and their people can actively participate in the process of culture building. What we need to do is develop a simple diagnostic and remedial approach which focuses on the interface between the individual and the organisation, an approach which directly involves all stakeholders in the process of change.

Another common but false assumption is that culture change as an initiative that must be led solely from the top, whose impact will then filter down throughout an organisation. This too is a message widely reinforced by management consultancies. If we follow this line of reasoning, encouraging leaders to take responsibility for something so ill-defined, nebulous and within the realm of expert practitioners inevitably puts them in a difficult position. In many cases, their response to being placed in this predicament is entirely predictable. The typical reaction of senior leadership is to appoint a *Head of culture* without a great deal of consideration about what the role entails. This is usually a mid-level Human Resource generalist without budget or decision-making latitude reporting into the HR hierarchy. These individuals often sit a long way from a position of direct influence on leadership and without the access or resources to make any real difference. Another increasingly common response is to rebrand HR Director role as *Director of People and Culture* a cosmetic change with essentially no meaningful alteration to the job description or responsibilities. This devalues the importance of understanding and managing culture and makes the task of change more difficult. This is simply because culture is created by everyone across an organisation who all need to be made part of the solution. Key to the emergence and maintenance of culture is the experience of each individual. Identifying an 'owner' of culture is a very effective way to undermine the relevance and validity of individual experience and reduce the likelihood of generalised participation in the process of change. People are also much less likely to contribute to the dialogue about culture if there is an 'expert' in the room, directly stifling their ability to focus on individual experience and its role in acculturation.

All too often the word culture is only used within organisations during change programmes or when things go wrong. This must change. What's needed, rather than one-off initiatives, is an ongoing endeavour with a focus on increasing the level of self-awareness of how culture exerts its effects on everyone. Authenticity is impossible without self-awareness, and people are developing ever more finely tuned authenticity detectors, which explains why cynicism regarding business, the media and politicians is at hitherto unprecedented levels. This means the need to embark on a continuous process of developing and maintaining conscious cultural

INTRODUCTION

self-awareness has never been more pressing as it is the only reliable way for informing what needs to change.

The power of culture to influence behaviour lies in the fact that in most situations it operates subtly. This is not because culture is inherently unknowable, but because we are not attuned to the collective behavioural assumptions it creates. Bring these into the collective consciousness and you take away its power. But the act of building self-awareness is not merely necessary for facilitating culture change, it is the very process of culture change. A healthy culture is in large part one where people routinely talk about culture, not in any self-deludingly aspirational way, but with regular scrutiny of why people do and don't do what they do or don't do. In this way, the underlying and often unconscious assumptions that drive behaviours can be discussed and if necessary, challenged and reframed and where the barriers that prevent anyone from exhibiting the desirable behaviours can be identified and removed. Self-awareness is a prerequisite of authenticity as much for organisations as for individuals. Most importantly, developing cultural self-awareness will mean people will do the right things more often and will allow organisations to avoid the worst financial and reputational damage when things go wrong, which they inevitably will from time to time.

What's needed is a fundamental shift in the way we view culture and how it can change. External consultants or subject matter experts can never 'fix' cultures. Given that our institutions are self-organising entities, any attempt to externally diagnose what needs to be done and to redesign programmes which focus on changing structures and processes will ultimately fail. There need be no project team or plan, no defined change programme other than a quest to build self-awareness and a creation of the conditions under which change can emerge through the process of self-reorganisation. For this to happen, it is essential to hold a mirror up to individuals and groups at all levels, right across an organisation. This makes a meaningful culture assessment, with simple, clear, and individually relevant outputs, central to the entire process.

While culture change certainly does need the direct involvement from senior management in terms of setting direction and tone to succeed, responsibility must be shared at every level if it is to be truly effective. The way most people experience culture, both employees and customers is at the local level, within their teams or departments. Culture is formed by collective behaviours of those within the immediate group, and this local culture is largely reinforced through the actions of local management and work colleagues. Everyone therefore must be involved and empowered in the change process if we want the right behaviours to spread. To achieve this, we need to be able to measure on a granular level and understand sub-cultures between departments and geographies and use this insight to identify and share best practices. Only by taking a consistent approach to assessment and learning at all levels can we diffuse the desired culture across an entire organisation.

Our large institutions are uniquely placed to be the catalysts for positive societal changes of all kinds and could help us address the challenges of environmental sustainability, inequality, and physical and mental wellbeing at work. The reality is however that they largely fail to do so, and their continued inability to understand and create the conditions where cultures can change remains a major barrier to progress. Culture is real, powerful and in no way optional as it is ubiquitous, a fundamental part of what makes us human. It defines and binds, it shapes our institutions and will determine our future. It influences the behaviour of everyone within a group, no matter how large or small. Its power lies in the fact that people unconsciously behave very differently when part of a group than they normally would as individuals. This could mean doing things that they would usually consider unthinkable, unethical, or immoral or conversely, it could also mean acting in ways which are driven by altruism and a greater sense

INTRODUCTION

of accountability and purpose. Despite its power to determine such critical outcomes, we consistently fail in our attempts to understand and change organisational culture. This is because much of what you have read or heard about organisational culture is lazy and wrong. It's time to question everything, especially what's said by business leaders, management consultancies, academics, and the media.

This book will introduce you to a simple and practical way of thinking about culture and how we can measure it and create the conditions under which change can happen naturally and organically. The strength of the approach we will explore lies in the fact that its simplicity makes it accessible to everyone, including time-poor managers and front-line employees. This allows everyone to be actively participate in the process of change, something without which most transformation initiatives can and do fail. If you're in the business of measuring or changing culture, it will provide a methodology for designing assessments and change programmes that really work, if not, then hopefully it will challenge some of your assumptions and show you how everyone can play an active part in the solution.

1

GOOSE OR STARLING?
How organisational cultures work

In 2014, Merriam-Webster dictionary declared culture its word of the year. It had seen a 15% increase in searches on the dictionary company's website and app year-on-year. This indicates two obvious things. The first is that people were using or encountering the word more frequently. The second that they were searching for a definition as they were unclear as to what it meant. It is debatable whether this situation has changed much since then, so an obvious place to start is to look for a commonly accepted definition of organisational culture. Even a very cursory search will be enough to tell you that there really isn't one. At first glance, there does seem to be some degree of consistency between the many of definitions out there but somehow, they all seem to fall short. They range from the unhelpfully vague and all-encompassing to the pedantically specific. The most commonly quoted definition, usually attributed to Charles Handy is;

> 'Culture is the way we do things around here'

At first sight, it may seem to fall into the category of unhelpfully vague, but while not perfect, this definition is simple, practical, and reasonably instructive. It reflects nearly all the most important aspects of culture; *do*, it's all about behaviours; *we*, it's about the collective, but also the individual; *way*, it has a qualitative aspect, it's not just what we do but how we do it, and; *here*, it's defined by consistent behaviours across a local group. What I particularly like about this definition is that it implies a circularity, as it hints at the self-reinforcing nature of culture. We do things this way because this is the way we do things, and we don't do them any other way because that's not what we do. Feedback loops of this kind are a fundamental feature of how culture works. Culture is inherently self-reinforcing, and we will explore many specific examples of this circularity in this book. An understanding of how these feedback loops work is of vital importance because changing culture is difficult or impossible without disrupting them.

If you're looking for something truly unhelpfully vague and all-encompassing this definition, so common, it's impossible to attribute to one single individual, is difficult to beat.

'Culture is everything'

Sure, culture can indeed exert its influence pretty much every aspect of an organisation and its people, but this is not the same as saying culture is everything. It is a failure to grasp this distinction that has reinforced the view that culture is a horribly huge and complex beast and has led to the development of impractical culture assessment tools which have a dizzying number of dimensions and indices.

Now for something more pedantically specific.

> '*Organisational culture represents the collective values, beliefs and principles of organisational members. It may also be influenced by factors such as history, type of product, market, technology, strategy, type of employees, management style, and national culture. Culture includes the*

25

organization's vision, values, norms, systems, symbols, language, assumptions, environment, location, beliefs and habits.'

International Journal of Applied Research 2017

The above highlights a real problem with the more specific definitions. It is the more precise they attempt to be, the longer and more all-encompassing they get. Essentially, they often list so many different elements they end up saying pretty much the same thing as *culture is everything* albeit in a different way. What both these kinds of definitions do is to reinforce the view that culture has so many intertwined elements as to render it unmeasurable and unmanageable. With all these elements, how could we possibly disentangle these interacting factors to get a clear view of what we need to change in any controllable way?

These more recent attempts to define culture show how since the relatively simple early definitions there has been an unnecessary overcomplication. They have spawned a proliferation of models of culture which have mostly taken us away from a simple understanding of its true nature. Models are a mainstay of the behavioural sciences and the stock in trade of management consultancies. They mostly tend to consist of labelled boxes, usually of different colours, linked to other boxes in various configurations by any number of lines and arrows. In an academic or consulting context, these representations are supposed to aid understanding of abstract ideas and relationships. In many cases however, they do nothing of the sort.

You will encounter a number of analogies, stories and anecdotes in this book, but I will not be referring to any models in an attempt to elucidate my views on culture. This is because I believe that models are in effect castrated analogies, bereft of their power to evoke, stripped of their ability to explain a concept in simple and powerful terms. Models tend to obfuscate and obscure. When deployed by HR Consultancies trying to sell their wares, in many cases there is little utility to them other than to provide false academic credentialisation or pseudo-intellectualisation. I know this through personal experience. Many years ago, I made the mistake of working for one of these consultancies and very early on was told by a Managing Partner in no uncertain terms that ideas and approaches alone were nothing. Nobody would part with any money for anything unless you had a model. This could be a simple two by two matrix a trusty fallback in any circumstance, but ideally something much more complex, with greater power to bamboozle. It didn't matter if the model was based on anything real, it just had to look plausible. I have heard this sentiment expressed by many others in various ways enough times since then, albeit mostly in less overtly cynical terms, to know that my innate distrust of models is well-founded. The truth is that models are to analogies what rules and instructions are to stories. If you want someone to grasp a concept, don't show them a model, give them a good analogy. If you want to encourage people to behave in a particular way, don't issue a rule-based instruction, tell them a good story. Having said that, it would still be instructive to have a brief overview of the murky and confused world of models of culture.

Models can have two functions. They can be academic, intended to help purely in the process of describing culture, or applied, having a clear practical purpose, for example being designed to be used in organisational contexts to facilitate culture assessment and change. It is this second type of model that we will focus on here. I am including this brief review, not to provide any critique of the relative merits of each, but to illustrate the bewildering array of models and the lack of consistency between them. Broadly, there are two types of applied cultural model. The first is typological, which typically describe a number of distinct types of organisational culture. The second is dimensional, which assume that culture can be seen as a multidimensional set of different interacting elements.

An example of a typological model comes from Charles Handy, who identified four distinct cultural types. The *Power Culture*, which revolves around a single central source of power in the organisation who initiates and co-ordinates the actions of those around them. This cultural type often exists within smaller organisations such as start-ups and privately owned businesses. The *Role Culture* which is primarily bureaucratic in nature where influence is distributed amongst specialists in their field. This is typified by traditional, stable businesses such as retail banks and other large corporations. In a *Role Culture*, job descriptions, titles, rules, and procedures are of primary importance. The third is *Task Culture*, where high performance and the achievement of results is the main consideration. Finally, the *Person Culture* is exemplified by consulting or legal practices where a loose and flexible structure exists within which individuals are more self-oriented, allocating work for themselves on their own terms, with mutual consent determining the best interests of a group.

Other examples include Deal and Kennedy, (1982) who describe four types of culture, namely *Work hard/play hard, Macho/tough guy, Process* and *Bet the company cultures*. Wallach (1983) described three distinct types of organisational culture, *Bureaucratic, Innovative* and *Supportive*. Cameron and Quinn (2011) described four, *Clan, Adhocracy, Market* and *Hierarchy.*

As for dimensional models of culture, there's a similar array.

Cooke and Lafferty (1987) described three dimensions- *Constructive, Passive/defensive* and *Aggressive/defensive.*

Hofstede (1984) initially identified four; *Power Distance, Individualism, Masculinity* and *Uncertainty avoidance*, although he was later to add two more.

Denison and Mishra (1995) described four dimensions, *Involvement, Consistency, Adaptability* and *Mission.*

Trompenaars and Hampden-Turner (1997) went for seven- *Universalism versus Particularism, Individualism versus Communitarianism, Specific versus Diffuse, Neutral versus Emotional, Achievement versus Ascription, Sequential time versus Synchronous time* and *Internal direction versus Outer direction.*

GOOSE OR STARLING?

Ashkanasy et al. (2000) trumped the lot of them with 10; *Leadership, Structure, Innovation, Job performance, Planning, Communication, Environment, Humanistic workplace, Development of individual* and *Socialization on entry*.

There are many more models out there, but I will spare you the details. As you can see, there has been something of a psychological feeding frenzy around defining models of culture with little consensus having been reached over the last 40 years. In fairness, most descriptive academic models have been developed using what are generally considered sound psychometric principles and rigorously tested for reliability and validity. The problem is that in many cases applied models have been enthusiastically embraced by management consultancies who have developed their own. These often start with lists of words or phrases, a brain dump of everything that culture could conceivably apply to, many incorporated from other existing models. A list is of course just a list and lists impress nobody. When you arrange these words and phrases, label them as dimensions or typologies into a diagram using different shapes and colours however, usually resulting in something that looks like a psychedelic spider's web, then hey presto, you've got yourself a model! This kind of process has resulted in many commonly used models consisting of 30 or more individual dimensions. Now that is certainly something with the power to bamboozle.

So which model of the more established models is right? Well take your pick. Which one you choose depends very much on the purpose for which you want to put it to. If you want to take an academic approach and identify through critical evaluation the one, or elements of each, that most accurately reflect the real world, in which case there's plenty to keep you busy. If you want to take an applied approach and develop a practical framework for measuring and changing culture, which is what we would normally wish to do, there is an obvious problem. Any framework should rightly be judged on its utility, on its ability to practically support culture change, but unfortunately it is beyond dispute that we have an awful track record of success in this regard. Why is our record so poor? Is this due to shortcomings of the models themselves or in their application? In practice, these two things are indivisible. The recurring problem is that none of these models presents culture in a way that is intuitively comprehensible to everyone, which they need to be if we are to get everyone on board. In most cases, assessment and change tools based on these models are required to be supplemented by reams of explanatory supporting text and, in some cases, entire books, without which they are tough to practically deploy and interpret. Under these circumstances, how can we realistically expect the vast majority to participate in the process of change?

The dimensions within models are often the product of a statistical technique commonly used in the social sciences called factor analysis. This is a multivariate analysis which has been extensively used in the exploration of the nature of personality. Factor analysis essentially takes a huge amount of data and correlates each data point against each of the others to identify underlying patterns of association. The result of this is a simplification of the data through the identification of a number of factors, which essentially define groups of related attributes. The analysis produces a range of possible solutions, it is the job of the statistician to determine which solution makes the most sense and how best to label these different factors. This technique has most famously been instrumental in establishing a broad consensus about what the main elements of personality are. These of course have come to be known as the Big 5, *Openness to experience, Conscientiousness, Extraversion, Agreeableness,* and *Neuroticism.* Many models of culture have also been derived using factor analytical techniques and the dimensions described in the most widely used models, such as those of Handy, Hofstede and Cameron & Quinn, closely mirror these personality factors.

GOOSE OR STARLING?

The idea that culture can be viewed as organisational personality may initially seem like a seductive one, and this is indeed how many consultancies characterise culture. The problem is that organisations are not like individuals, they do not have largely immutable personality dimensions which direct their behaviour and decision making in a predictable way over long periods of time. By contrast, cultures are defined purely by behaviour which is almost infinite in its variety and constantly in flux, changing in response to internal and external pressures. Neither are cultures simple aggregates of all the individuals that make them up. They have almost infinite flexibility and, as we will see, can and do have overall cultural characteristics which are completely different from the sum of their individual parts. Just consider Mid Staffs. What personality variables or combination thereof could account for the catastrophic failures there? What could possibly make one group of dedicated health and support professionals behave so differently from virtually every other seemingly identical group across the NHS? Certainly not some kind of aggregate of individual personalities. The organisational personality analogy is also extremely unhelpful if we're looking to change culture. Personality traits do of course exert a strong influence on individual behaviour, but they are fixed and change little throughout an entire lifetime. If we were to take the organisational personality analogy to its logical conclusion, this would mean that to change culture we would need a complete change in personnel to better reflect the culture we're looking to achieve. This is of course neither practical nor possible.

But there is a bigger problem with each of these models. There is one essential quality of culture that each of these definitions fails to incorporate, and it is illustrated by the following simple story.

Two tadpoles were swimming along when suddenly a frog swims past them and says;

'The water's lovely today isn't it'

As the frog swims on, one tadpole turns to the other and says;

'The what's lovely?'

This is a story that's been told many times in many different versions and contexts, but it illustrates something of fundamental importance when considering culture. We're all immersed in it, most often to the extent that we don't even know it's there. It exerts a powerful effect on everything we do and how we see the world, but unless we have the ability to see it for what it is from an objective perspective, we are at its mercy. Of course, the amphibious frog has experience of living in and out of water and can move from pond to pond, so has the capacity to recognise the water quality as other, as distinct and different. It can distinguish between water of different types and knows when it's lovely and when it's not. The tadpoles have no such perspective. At least not yet. How could they? This is not because there is anything about water which is inherently intangible or unknowable. It is because they have never experienced anything else, and consequently have never asked themselves even the most fundamental questions about the substrate in which they live. The tadpoles lack even the most basic awareness about their environment. The same can be said for most members of organisations in relation to culture in that they lack cultural self-awareness. This prevents them from asking important questions about how their work environment influences so much of what they think and do.

Organisational psychologist Edgar Schein gave us a very simple means of conceptualising this important characteristic of culture early on. He used an analogy, and one that you will almost certainly be familiar with. It was clear and simple and like all analogies was not perfect, but it did encapsulate many of the most important elements of culture. It was that culture is like an iceberg. What you can see above the surface is only 10%- the vast majority is below the surface, out of sight, but it is the 90% that lies below the surface that really matters. What's above the surface is obvious, but unreliable and can give you a false sense of security as it gives no clue as to the hidden jagged ice that can rip open your hull and consign you to the depths. This does not mean that what lies beneath is unknowable. It does mean however that you have to look at the iceberg in a different way if you want to understand it fully. Take the time and effort to look below the surface and you get the full picture and will be much better able to steer a secure course.

Schein asserted that the visible portion of the iceberg consists of two parts. The first is made up of artifacts, the visible trappings of culture. These include things like dress, language, hierarchies, titles, and physical surroundings for example. Many organisations attempt to exemplify their culture, especially in terms of employer branding, by emphasising perks like concierge services, flexitime, and free breakfasts. These are great examples of artifacts. Sure, these can signal the kind of culture you're striving to achieve, but do not make the mistake of believing that these constitute culture itself or even have any power to create the culture you aspire to. In fact, these will only be seen as window dressing if they are at odds with the true deep culture that people experience in their daily work. This kind of mismatch will in all probability make those you really need and want to keep head for the exit.

The second constituent part of the visible portion of the iceberg is made up of what Schein called espoused values. These are the things that an organisation says about its culture and ways of working. Espoused values include things that the organisation says about itself, leadership communications and employer brand. While they provide some insight into an organisation's culture in terms of aspiration, they are inherently unreliable. This is because of the common mismatch between what an organisation says it stands for, and what it demonstrates it values through how its people behave. These are deeper indicators and levers of culture than artifacts, but pale into insignificance compared to what lies below the surface.

COUNTING THE DANCE STEPS

The majority of the iceberg and what lies beyond direct observation is made up of implicit assumptions. These are underlying beliefs held by members of an organisation and are significantly more reliable indicators of an organisation's culture than either artifacts or espoused values as they directly influence how people actually behave. A great example of how implicit assumptions differ from espoused values is that while many organisations will say they promote an environment where employees can speak up and challenge the way things are done, many employees will however still be reluctant to do so because they harbour an implicit assumption that to do so risks being labelled a troublemaker. Implicit assumptions are the most reliable indicator of actual culture and bringing these into the conscious realm and challenging them provides the most direct route to changing it.

More recently, Schein's analogy has been revised and refined in order to more accurately reflect the true nature of culture. In the book *Organizational Culture and Leadership,* by Edgar and his son Peter Schein, the three levels of culture are retained but culture is described as being analogous to a lily pond. The flowers and lily pads above the water's surface are the visible artifacts and espoused values which are created and nourished by what lies beneath. In this way, the implicit assumptions can be seen as more akin to a dynamic system rather than inert and sterile ice. This means that culture can be influenced through the creation of conditions which change the underlying dynamics of the system. These conditions (seeds, water quality and fertilizer for example) are described as being limited in number, as are the key assumptions that govern culture.

Schein's analogy is a very good one and has become extremely influential. According to Schein, employees unconsciously adapt to their cultural environment to enjoy a successful and stress-free work life. Those who do not, or are unable to become disenchanted, demotivated and often leave. If you don't feel personally or professionally that you are able to thrive within a particular culture, you can either adapt your behaviour, hunker down and weather it or vote with your feet. As we will see, this has profound implications for the ability of organisations to succeed through inclusion, innovation, and effective risk management. The characteristic behavioural responses to various different cultural conditions also provide us with a practical framework with which to measure culture in a simple and meaningful way.

For anyone seeking to measure and manage culture, all the definitions and models of culture ultimately fall short because they are attempts at answering the wrong question. What we need to be asking is not *what is culture*? rather it has to be *how does culture work*? Let's use another very simple analogy. A car can be accurately defined as a mechanical means of personal transportation, but a functional definition like this tells us nothing about what to do when it goes wrong or when we need to give it a tune up. To do this we need to know how it works. And we don't usually need to know how the whole thing works, just the bit we're trying to fix. If the brakes don't work or are sticking, there's little benefit in swatting up on the functioning of the electrics, carburettor, or exhaust system. The same holds for culture. We can define what culture is in the generalised sense, we can also list all of the component parts, but what this gives us is a long list of everything that culture might be able to influence. This is how many have ended up with models consisting of such an unmanageable number of elements. Schein's iceberg analogy has the distinct advantage over the other definitions as it begins to describe how culture actually works. Until you understand the process through which cultures are established, propagated and reinforced, you will never be able to change them. Luckily for us, the possible fundamental building blocks of culture were postulated over 40 years ago and tellingly, not by a psychologist but a biologist. They're called memes and were first described by Professor Richard Dawkins in his seminal book The Selfish Gene.

COUNTING THE DANCE STEPS

'A meme is an idea, behaviour, or style that spreads from person to person within a culture. A meme acts as a unit for carrying cultural ideas, symbols, or practices that can be transmitted from one mind to another through writing, speech, gestures, rituals, or other imitable phenomena'

Richard Dawkins postulated that memes are analogous to genes in that they carry information, are readily transmitted from person to person, are stable but can mutate and convey an adaptive advantage or disadvantage to their hosts. Within an organisational context, memes take root and propagate themselves largely without the host being aware and have no regard for organisational strategy or cultural aspirations. Dawkins did not introduce the idea of the meme with the intention of launching an entire new field of inquiry. It was an analogy exploring the possibility that natural selection could apply to situations beyond evolutionary biology and be used to conceptualise different kinds of evolution in a more general sense. Nonetheless, his analogy has gained traction and has spawned a new area of study called memetics.

Critics of Dawkins have been quick to point to what they consider an inherent flaw in his thinking in that genes are concrete physical entities. While biological evolution requires genes to be the physical agents of information transmission, culture must be propagated in a very different way. If culture spreads from person to person, how can it do this if it is beyond anyone's capacity to see it, hear it or feel it? By telepathy? By some insidious process like a virus infecting an oblivious host? The viral analogy has been employed by Richard Dawkins himself to illustrate the unconscious and self-interested way culture spreads, but there is an obvious shortcoming with it. This is that there is no material agent by which culture can spread virally as there is no actual physical virus. This is not a criticism of his use of this analogy, no analogy is perfect. What it is however, is a great illustration of how the imperfections of any analogy can help to shed light on the truth. As there is no physical vector of transmission and yet culture clearly does spread from one person to another. By definition therefore, it cannot do so completely subliminally. So, what is the process through which cultures propagate themselves?

Very simply, acculturation happens through the interplay of behaviours and the collective assumed consequences of those behaviours. Our own behaviour, and observation of the behaviours of others, leads to the formation of assumptions that are very powerful determinants of future behaviour. These are all perfectly tangible but more often than not, we don't consciously notice the transmission process because its effects are subtle, and we are not attuned to them. This opens the possibility that we can become so just by asking ourselves a few basic questions, through examining our assumptions, through scrutinising what drives our behaviours and those of others. This is a habit and a learned skill, but it is one that very few of us apply in our working lives. This skill is cultural self-awareness, and we will be returning to this concept many times. Memetics has not widely been applied in the assessment and management of organisational culture, but it opens a whole new possibility for a practical paradigm for understanding culture and change. Unmask the assumptions driving key behaviours and you take away the power of memes and put it in your own hands.

What matters most in defining organisational culture is behaviour. Behaviours which are assumed to convey an advantage to individuals will more readily be adopted than those that don't. This is particularly true in organisational settings where your chances of success or progression largely lie in the hands of managers or supervisors. When these assumptions become shared across large numbers of people, they lead to the collective behaviours that define culture. Consequently, we can describe the building blocks of culture as the collective assumptions about the consequences of specific actions. In their simplest form, these shared assumptions take the form of; If I/you/they do this…then this will happen

If I voice my concerns about how we're treating our customers, I'll be labelled a troublemaker

If I take a risk and implement that new idea, it will be held against me if it doesn't work out

If I promote John to that managerial position, it's a huge risk. He's not like anyone else in the leadership team. Making that call could come back to bite me

I call these building blocks behaviour memes, and while these behaviour-assumed consequence pairings operate largely at an unconscious level, when you start looking for them, they're everywhere. The great thing about the concept of behaviour memes is that it provides a simple and readily understandable view of how culture is created and reinforced. It also provides a clear framework by which culture can be consciously changed. Bring the core assumptions into the conscious realm, change the consequences of the behaviours they reinforce visibly and consistently, reframe the collective assumptions, and you have permanently changed culture. Creating the conditions under which this can happen inevitably takes consistency and persistence, but it provides a simple and measurable roadmap to success. It also allows you to focus on a manageable number of key behaviours that define any specific attribute of culture you're looking to change. These examples also show how culture does not just exert its influence on passive recipients and is not just something that is done to you. It has its embodiment in your own actions and decisions as much as the decisions made about you. If we reframe those negative assumptions we listed earlier, they could equally become;

If I voice my concerns about how we're treating our customers, together we can work out a way of improving the quality of service.

If I take a risk and implement that new idea, if it doesn't work out, we'll chalk it up to experience, learn from it and move on.

GOOSE OR STARLING?

If I promote John to that managerial position, it'll enhance the diversity of the leadership team. That has to be a good thing.

The important point here is that culture is about behaviours which are all perfectly observable, measurable, and amenable to change. But before we discuss how we might begin to change culture, we really need explore the practical mechanism by which culture is created, reinforced and sustained in greater detail.

The practical definition of culture from a behaviour meme perspective is that culture consists of the collective behaviours and the shared assumptions that drive them within a group. A very simple example of this as if you and your colleagues see someone being shot down at a meeting for questioning your boss, you will be very unlikely to speak up and do so yourself in the future. Similarly, if you never see anyone questioning the boss you could easily come to the same conclusion and, rightly or wrongly conclude that it wouldn't be a good idea. So, the consequences, real or perceived, that you infer from a situation drive the behaviours themselves. If negative consequences are associated with that behaviour, you just aren't going to do it and when these behaviour-assumed consequence pairings are shared across a large number of people, they come to constitute culture. What's more, when assumptions and behaviours become shared in this way, they become entirely self-reinforcing. When people don't speak up, this reinforces the collective assumption that speaking up would not be a good idea, which in turn prevents people from speaking up and so on. Once formed, behaviour memes also reinforce the assumptions which we use to attribute meaning to future events, particularly when there is possible ambiguity. For example, if we already harbour an assumption that speaking up in public and challenging leadership is not a great idea, we a likely to be quick to interpret a clearly disgruntled colleague not doing so as due to a concern on their part that the personal consequences will be negative for them. If we believe that a culture of open feedback holds sway, we may be more likely to attribute this to the fact that their differences have already been resolved in another way out of the public eye. The existence of this type of feedback loop operating largely unconsciously and subtly, helps to explain why culture can be so resistant to change. It also clearly highlights the path to the most effective way of changing culture, namely bringing the assumptions driving behaviour into the collective consciousness in order to disrupt these self-reinforcing feedback loops. As we will see, this way of conceptualising culture also gives us an objective and valid way of measuring it.

Let's look at another example. I've just joined a company I'm looking around and I'm highly sensitised to everything around me, consciously and unconsciously absorbing a lot of things about my new working environment. Naturally I want to succeed both personally and professionally, and I'm looking for cues about how to best make this happen. I will be asking myself from fundamental questions about how I'm going to get on in this environment and how I'm going to make a success of it. One such question is;

If I want to succeed here what do I need to do, do I keep my head down or do I do what I can to stand out, get my elbows and try and make a difference?

Your choice of a course of action will undoubtedly depend upon a number of factors, but a large part of the difference in behavioural response will inevitably be down to implicit assumptions, specifically those we make about the extent to which we feel comfortable and secure in our new work setting. These we pick up largely from the behaviours of everyone around us, leaders, managers and colleagues and the stories we hear about the consequences of different possible courses of action. In some instances, we may be responding to the observed consequences of others' behaviour and in others, direct experience of the consequences of our own actions. In an environment where an individual feels secure and comfortable with a strong sense of belonging to the group, in other words, as part of an inclusive culture, they are much more likely to exhibit the behaviours which help them to stand out relative to their peers. This means speaking up and voicing concerns, challenging the status quo, articulating innovative ideas and taking considered risks to implement them. These are all behaviours that mitigate against the kinds of organisational failures we see too regularly. If I belong, I'm not going to get shot for getting myself out there, the personal risk is low, and I am in fact likely to benefit from taking that approach.

If we view culture in this way, behaviours give the lie to the assumptions we are making and affectively define the culture. Culture is no longer a dark and intangible force, lurking behind the scenes exerting its malign influence. Instead, it becomes measurable and manageable. Differences between cultures are clearly exhibited by the quantifiably different behavioural responses of the people operating within a range of organisational contexts. Specific aspects of culture can be observed through the precise behaviours that exemplify them. Everyone can be involved in the dialogue of change when what's being measured and managed is expressed in simple behavioural terms which are relevant and accessible to all. Change can be tracked over time and best practices can be identified and shared. Forget about Jungian Archetypes, forced categorisations of cultural typology or complex models derived from multivariant analysis. It's purely and simply about the interplay between shared assumptions and collective behaviours. Inclusive cultures hold the key to facilitating the behaviours that inoculate an organisation against a range of internal and external threats. If the old analogy that diversity is being invited to the party and inclusion is being asked to dance is true then, if we want an objective and quantitative measure of the inclusiveness of a culture, don't ask people if they've enjoyed the party, simply count the dance steps. To extend the analogy, if you want to create the right culture it's no good trying to mandate dancing or issuing instructions about how and when to dance, simply put the right music on.

COUNTING THE DANCE STEPS

The truth is that when entering a new working environment, many people are likely to err on the side of caution in terms of their behaviour. It's easy to see the safest option, at least at the outset, as to keep your head down until you have a better understanding of the lay of the land. The potential problem here is that assumptions formed, and behaviours adopted early on become difficult to change over time because they are entirely self-reinforcing. This means that providing an inclusive environment is not a passive endeavour and cannot just be about removing barriers to the kinds of behaviours we need to see. It is about actively taking steps to encourage and incentivise desirable behaviours, particularly during employees' early careers with their employer when behaviour memes are first beginning to take root. Anticipating that newcomers will be undergoing this process of meme acquisition provides us with an obvious opportunity to start the process of building cultural awareness early on.

It's often said that while anyone can copy your strategy, nobody can copy your culture. This feeds the narrative that culture is infinite in variety and too impossibly complex to replicate. It also implies that culture can only be understood when considered in its entirety, and that it is not possible to isolate discrete elements of culture that can be copied and integrated. Looking at culture in terms of fundamental building blocks like behaviour memes shows that this does not have to be the case. This view of culture also illustrates how, while there may not be a single good culture, there are certainly desirable and undesirable behaviour memes, and these will be the same across very different organisations even if they have different strategic objectives. The oft repeated platitude that no two cultures are the same is true, but this is only because a culture is not a single unified entity, it is an array of building blocks, a behavioural memeplex.

The meme complex, or memeplex is an integrated network of complimentary memes. If you're wondering how something as seemingly complex and nuanced as culture can be explained in such simple terms as behaviour memes, like literally everything else, it is this integration of a large number of very simple building blocks that creates complexity. To extend Dawkins' metaphor, memeplexes are analogous to gene complexes found together on chromosomes as they are groups of memes that are commonly found coexisting. They reinforce one another, making them better able to successfully propagate themselves. This is one more characteristic of cultures which makes them resistant to change. One important way in which memeplexes differ from gene complexes however is that they are not passed down through generations. This hints at the possibility for changing them in a much shorter time frame. Another is that unlike gene complexes, memeplexes do not require their hosts to benefit from them in order to proliferate. Behaviour memes just have to be implicitly and collectively assumed to contribute to individual success to become successful themselves. In this way, memes that are unhealthy or damaging are perfectly capable of propagating and persisting, and indeed often do.

If a memetic view still strikes you as too narrow a way to look at culture, let's revisit the more pedantic of the definitions.

'...culture includes the organization's vision, values, norms, rituals, stories, systems, symbols, language, assumptions, beliefs and habits.'

Vision and values are expressions of shared assumptions about the right way to behave. Norms are shared assumptions about expected collective behaviours. Rituals are repeated formalised behaviours with symbolic significance. Stories, both current and historical, systems and symbols are important because they create or reinforce the shared assumptions that drive collective behaviours. Whichever way we look at many of the constituent parts those long and pedantic definitions of culture we circle back to the same key elements. Assumptions and behaviours, just as Schein asserted.

Another ubiquitous and enduring myth about culture which a memetic view could mistakenly be seen to reinforce is that if change happens through evolution rather than revolution, it can therefore happen only gradually and slowly. While it is true that evolution is only observable at a macro level, the local individual experience of cultural change is most often revolutionary. We also know that cultures start to develop quickly within newly formed groups. This hints at the possibility for changing cultures in a relatively short period of time. How long does it take to change culture? Well in essence, this question is how long does it take to change collective assumptions and behaviours within a particular group in a sustainable way? The answer has to be, under the right circumstances not very long. Create the right conditions and behaviours and the assumptions that reinforce them will change, maintain those conditions and the change will stick. Culture change is most often not something that is experienced by the individual as a gradual process of attenuation and adaptation, in most cases it is rapid enough to be painful and destabilising and if it is not, then you can be pretty sure no real change is happening. The fact that change inevitably takes people out of their comfort zones is one that is consistently recognised in all the commonly used change management models.

While culture change is not easy or painless, it certainly need not be glacial. As evolutionary geneticists are increasingly aware, evolution in species happens in a series of jumps. For many millennia, nothing will happen, then when the conditions are right, change happens in a flurry and when you consider the timeframes, a mad rush. Similarly, if you create the right conditions in organisations, put the right music on, then change can also be rapid. Given the urgency created by a constantly changing business and social environment, in the modern world it absolutely needs to be. Many organisations however continue to enter into change programme with a defeatist mindset that says it will be a long slog and one whose impact will be impossible to quantify within short or even medium timescales. Others are deterred from even making a start.

GOOSE OR STARLING?

Another area where the prevailing narrative is questionable is the extent to which we can or can't define what good looks like in terms of culture. The notion of a 'good' culture is typically characterised as being fraught with problems. Conventional wisdom states that the acid test is the extent to which a culture supports or undermines an organisation's ability to achieve its strategic objectives. This by implication means that there are as many possible good cultures as there are possible organisational strategies. There are behaviours and competencies that when widely shared are indicators of what we could reasonably call a high-performance culture, and these appear to be largely universal. They are pretty much the same irrespective of your strategic objectives or which aspect of culture you are focusing on. This will become clearer when we discuss the issues of risk, inclusion, and innovation in detail later in this book. Nevertheless, your chosen priority focus must be governed by the most pressing issues impacting your ability to succeed as a business. This must be the starting point for any measurement and change programme.

When people attempt to define what a good culture looks like they almost exclusively think about it from an organisational perspective, in terms of process and practice, benefits or perks. This is in many ways natural as these things are tangible and obvious and can undoubtedly attract people to a particular employer. Some will be more appropriate in certain work settings than in others, but the question we need to be asking is to what extent is it possible to identify common cultural elements that all organisations should strive for? In order to start doing this, let's look at the problem from a different angle, from the perspective of the individual. When we do this, we shift our focus onto the capacity of the organisation to fulfil the different motivations, needs and aspirations their people may have. Thinking about this in the context of a hierarchy of needs, the most basic building block of a good culture has to be to the extent to which it provides a safe and secure working environment, not just in terms of physical but also psychological safety. Above this could be providing the opportunity to act independently; Autonomy, the ability to make a positive difference; Purpose, or to learn and grow to be able to do something to the best of their abilities; Mastery, or to feel a sense of belong to a cohesive group; Relatedness. If we look at culture in this way, a good culture can be described as one with the capacity to satisfy a clearly defined range of basic human needs and intrinsic motivators.

When we think about an ideal culture from both an organisational and an individual perspective we find that the two are almost entirely complementary in terms of the behaviours and the corresponding assumptions that we want to support. What's more, these are consistent across many different outcomes that we might look to achieve. In other words, what's good for the individual is good for the organisation, and the way people behave when they feel a certain way is very consistent and predictable, no matter what your strategic objectives or cultural starting point may be. When people feel safe and secure with a strong sense of belonging within a group something amazing happens. They start doing the things that define a healthy culture and support mutually beneficial outcomes. They contribute, they ask questions, they challenge things and they come up with new ideas. They treat their colleagues with respect and expect to be treated the same. When they're unhappy or unsure about something speak up, they talk more openly about their feelings their aspirations and their concerns. They'll admit to their mistakes and speak about their values and those of the organisation. If a core purpose of any culture is to define and bind a group together for the mutual benefit of each of its members, a primary focus in building a healthy culture must be to provide a work environment that is in all aspects safe and secure for everyone, whatever kind of organisation you have. This won't mean that your people will always behave impeccably and do the right thing, nothing will ever guarantee that, but it will mean that your workplace will be more inclusive, your people will be more innovative, far better able to manage risk and to behave in line with your core values.

GOOSE OR STARLING?

In her book, *The Fearless Organization: Creating Psychological Safety in the Workplace for Learning, Innovation, and Growth,* Dr Amy Edmondson defined psychological safety at work as being characterised by the belief that you won't be punished or belittled for contributing new ideas, asking questions, expressing concerns, or admitting to making mistakes. This is the absolute exemplar of how shared assumptions can drive desirable collective behaviours, in other words a memeplex. Dr Timothy Clark added to this in his book *The 4 Stages of Psychological Safety: Defining the Path to Inclusion and Innovation,* by describing the process employees need to go through before they can fully contribute to organisational success. The first he terms *inclusion safety*. This is when people feel a sense of belonging within the group and a positive connection with its members, irrespective of who they are. The second is *learner safety*, which responds to the need for people to learn and develop personally and professionally. The third is *contributor safety*, which satisfies the desire for individuals to use their skills and knowledge to contribute to the best of their abilities and finally *challenger safety,* which enables people to make a positive difference through inspiring change. As we can see, these tick a lot of boxes in terms of the basic intrinsic motivators, relatedness, mastery, autonomy and purpose.

Like much of what is said about culture, assertions that it is not possible to define what a good culture looks like, there is no one size fits all solution, and that culture cannot be copied are misleading and lazy. Thanks to the work of Edmonson, Clark and others, we have the makings of a very compelling and detailed template for what the foundation of a good culture looks like. We can also identify key elements which can be replicated across very different organisations. When defined in terms of assumptions and behaviours, a desired culture can be created through the establishment of discrete building blocks. When we think about culture change in these terms, in many instances, the required number of critical behaviour changes, and therefore reframed assumptions, needed to reach a desired cultural state is far from daunting, it is actually manageably small.

When looking at the range of academic and practical definitions we can clearly see that culture is very likely to mean different things to different people. If we want to create a common frame of reference, we need to consider what different groups of people mean when they talk about it. The emphasis placed on culture by many academics and most management consultancies is on structures, process and hierarchies and how they influence behaviour. This is partly because it is the perspective that they understand best, but in the case of management consultancies, it is also because it allows them to expand the scope and cost of the work that they do. This is usually through upselling with the involvement of other service lines like organisational design, leadership development, talent management and reward. Leadership also tends to share this macro view of culture. Why wouldn't they? It's their perspective, how they see their relationship to their organisations every day. This means they look at the big things, the structures and processes, corporate communications, the high-level metrics. But this is not how most people experience culture and this mismatch has profound consequences for how we look to create change. A structural/process view of culture chimes with many business leaders as these are many of the more tangible levers that they traditionally look to pull to exert influence over their people. These are the terms of reference that leaders and consultants will typically use, but what do employees think about when they talk about culture in a work context?

This matters because it allows us to start answering some fundamental questions. Firstly, if we are looking to take a building blocks approach to culture change, where do we start and what are the basic foundations upon which we can build? If we are to understand the employee experience in relation to culture, where should we be focusing our attention? If we are to involve all employees in the process of change as we should aim to do, we need to get their buy in. To get their buy in we need to be speaking about and addressing culture from a perspective they identify with and believe is relevant to their working lives. When they think and talk about culture, what is their frame of reference, what issues related to their working lives are top of mind when thinking about culture?

The evidence shows that the employee perspective on culture is very different from that of leadership or traditional change agents such as external consultants. In a recent study by text analytics firm Organisation View, artificial intelligence was used to categorise the comments posted on a well-known employer rating website. This was done by iteratively 'training' the system to categorise each of the many hundreds of thousands of comments left on the site in terms of the topic or topics it addressed, one of which was organisational culture. The system also analysed the inter-relatedness of each of the topics mentioned by contributors, allowing the co-occurrence of different topics to be assessed and mapped. This effectively allowed the researchers to identify what other elements of their work experience people were referencing when they commented on their workplace culture. The results were consistent and clear. When people referenced culture, they tended not associate it with macro-organisational elements such as processes, structures or systems. Top of mind for them were not factors like reward, bureaucracy, career development or flexible working, but interpersonal elements much closer to them in their everyday work experience. These included relationships with colleagues, local leadership and management, teamwork, shared values and inclusion, elements which are consistently under-emphasised by leadership and management consultants when addressing culture. These interpersonal factors are not incidental or soft, they are fundamental to the development of a positive work culture and highlight the importance of focusing on individual experience first and foremost. This finding suggests that in attempting to influence culture through changing structures, procedures and systems, as we do time and time again, we are in fact merely treating the symptoms rather than the cause. These structures and processes are thing created and reinforced by the prevailing mindsets and behaviours that define culture, not the other way around. They are precisely the things Schein referred to as artifacts. If was accept this fact, then nothing can be achieved by way of lasting change without addressing the individual influences that really seem to drive people's behaviour in their workplaces, a fact that would go a long way to explain our historic failure to effectively manage culture.

A very common image that's often associated with leadership is that of a skein of geese. We often see the goose at the front with the others dutifully following in a perfect V-shape as analogous with leadership and followership. This is certainly how many CEOs would like to visualise their role as leaders, forging ahead and providing a clear sense of direction for the rest. In reality however, their companies are self-organising entities within which culture will inevitably emerge rather than be consciously created. In terms of culture, people within organisations are not like these compliant and predictable geese, they are more like starlings.

The common starling is an unremarkable bird in most respects, small, black, and rather generic. If you asked a six-year-old child to draw a typical bird, the chances are you'd get something that wouldn't look a million miles away from the humble starling. In most respects their behaviour is pretty unremarkable too, but when flocking in large numbers they can collectively transform into something truly extraordinary. Starlings often congregate at dusk to form intricately swirling, swooping, pulsating swarms often numbering many thousands of individuals. These gatherings are called murmurations and provide an unforgettably mesmeric display for anyone lucky enough to see one in action.

GOOSE OR STARLING?

The mechanics of the murmuration have been the subject of considerable research over the years. Early theorists believed that something as complex and beautiful could only come about through some kind of mysterious force, such as collective telepathy. More recent research has shown that although a murmuration may look like a coordinated whole, each individual bird is merely tracking the movement of its seven closest neighbours to the exclusion of everything else by following three simple rules.

1. If you're too close to a neighbour, move away
2. If you're too far away from a neighbour, move towards them
3. Fly in the same direction as your immediate neighbours

These basic rules, when followed by each individual, produce the beautiful and mesmerising complexity of the murmuration. The groups of seven overlap, meaning that movements are transmitted right across the flock in an organic and seamless way. This simple mechanism has been shown to model the movement of groups of creatures as diverse as wildebeest, fish and insects. As the expert in murmurations, Mario Pesendorfer of Vienna University puts it;

"There are two ways that you can elicit large group behaviour. You can have the top-down control, where you have some kind of leadership, or some kind of top-down mechanism. Think of a rock show, you have the rock star in the front and he starts clapping his hands, and the whole stadium starts clapping. But these murmurations are actually self-organising, meaning that it's the individual's little behavioural rules that make it scale up to the large group. In order to understand this behaviour, we have to go from the local scale — what is the individual doing, what are the rules that the individual is following?"

Collective group behaviour like this does of course have a distinct purpose as it confers considerable benefits to the individuals within the group. It takes a brave, or stupid bird to ignore its fellow starlings and set off on a path of its own. It risks

51

being separated from its comrades to find itself at the mercy of the hawks who patrol the fringes of the flock. It is believed that the mesmeric power of the murmuration confuses predators by making targeting and zeroing in on an individual much more difficult than would otherwise be the case. Closely matching the movements of its neighbours also means that an individual bird can respond to threats without ever needing to be aware of them. It just takes one neighbour to spot a hawk and take evasive action, or for it to mirror the behaviour of one of their neighbours who has done the same, to cause the individual to also avoid being eaten, even when it is completely unaware of the danger it's in. This individual's response will in turn then cause its neighbours to react.

As an analogy, murmurations work very well when applied to organisational culture. They illustrate how thinking of culture as something that's done to you is only part of the story. The actions of each individual are collectively responsible for creating, reinforcing or changing culture. It also shows how the least risky option can most often be seen as to do as your colleagues do. The parallels with organisational culture are obvious. Much as many of our business leaders would like to think of themselves as akin to the leader of the orchestra, whose every swoop and twitch of the baton is followed intently by each musician, we know the reality is very different. In organisations the result is much more the organised chaos of the murmuration rather than the coordinated harmony of a symphony, or a predictably V-shaped skein.

The individual birds are responding to local cues and have absolutely no knowledge of or consideration for the murmuration itself. The starlings are just doing what they do while inadvertently and collectively creating something much bigger than themselves, something much more intricate and powerful than the sum of its parts. In the same way, individuals within an organisation experience culture through personal interactions with a relatively small number of local managers and team members. Despite the fact that culture is formed by their collective behaviours with peers, most employees do not consider culture as something that they have any direct control over, let alone something they are actively creating through everything they do. They are also largely unaware of the profound impact that the behaviour of others is having on their own behaviour. The murmuration also provides a great example for anyone reluctant to consider it feasible for anything as seemingly complex as organisational culture to be distilled down to very simple building blocks. Murmurations show how individuals following a few very basic rules can, when operating as a group, readily produce something seemingly impossibly complex and unpredictably organic. The same is true for culture and everything else in the universe.

The principles which govern flocks of starlings also apply to certain species of fish. We have all seen those amazing images on programmes, usually voiced over by David Attenborough, of millions of anchovies gliding through the sea in shimmering shoals. We have also seen those shoals being mercilessly attacked from all sides by gannets, predatory fish, sea lions and most impressively, humpback whales who construct ever-decreasing circular curtains of bubbles that concentrate the shoal so that thousands of anchovies may be swallowed in a single gulp. This is when shoal becomes bait ball, when the advantages of sticking together become a distinct disadvantage, allowing predators the certainty of knowing precisely where and how to launch a coordinated attack. The unfortunate anchovies stick together to the last as they know no other way to behave, until the very last anchovy is consumed.

It is the failure to recognise the crucial point when shoal becomes bait ball, when their instinct to stick together becomes a liability rather than a benefit, that leads to collective calamity. This is because the anchovies' behaviour is driven by instinct and nothing else. People are of course different in that they have the capacity to adapt their behaviour when circumstances dictate but recognising what behaviour change is required and when is not always easy. Both awareness of the situation and awareness of the current behavioural deficiencies of the group is crucial in allowing both people and organisations to adapt to change. Without cultural self-awareness, many decisions will be reflex, conditioned responses, based on the narrow parameters of what we have always done around here. This stifles creativity and prevents the development of a capacity to adapt to new and unfamiliar circumstances. The formation of a bait ball is the fishy equivalent of circling the wagons. Neither tactic tends to turn out well.

2

MIMI'S STORY

It's Mimi's first day at work. She's excited, a little nervous but more than anything, she wants to make a good impression and succeed in her new workplace. Her eyes and ears are open, her antennae are scanning for every cue about how best to proceed. Consequently, she's either consciously, or more likely unconsciously, asking herself some pretty fundamental questions, like;

> *If I want to get on here, how should I behave, what should I do and what shouldn't I do?*

There are obviously many different possible courses of action that she might choose to take, but here's one example of a fundamental question she and many others in her position will be asking themselves;

> *Do I do what I can to fit in……..or……. do what I can to stand out?*

In most circumstances where do people fall? They want to do what they can to fit in right? It makes sense, it's much less risky and much more likely to serve them well in most work contexts, at least in the short term. Mimi is no different, she assumes the best way to behave is to go with the flow, keep her head down at least until she knows her way around a bit better. All natural, understandable and very, very common. Once the initial assumptions like Mimi's start to take root however, they can become difficult to shift. She has fallen under the influence of a behaviour meme. It is going to exert a powerful impact on her behaviours and decisions and in most circumstances, she's not even going to be aware of the effect it is having. At least it will help her to get ahead, won't it?

It's the day before Mimi's first big team meeting. Mimi overhears an experienced colleague complaining to another team member about the way client projects have been allocated. He clearly feels very aggrieved and blames the Team Manager. Apparently, he's going to publicly confront the Team Manager tomorrow at the meeting. This should be interesting.

During the meeting Mimi is a little nervous. The regular review of client projects is on the agenda, and she's on the edge of her seat. How is this going to play out? But the project review finishes, they're now on to the monthly forecasting and her disgruntled new colleague has said nothing. Imperceptibly another meme is seeded. It's obviously not such good idea to openly challenge the team leader, even if you are an experienced employee. It appeared that her new colleague was just venting, he had no intention of confronting his manager after all. If she were to do something like that as a new employee, just imagine what the consequences might be!

The new behaviour meme takes root quickly because it confirms her original decision. She was right to keep her head down. This is the beginning of the creation of a memeplex. But what Mimi doesn't know is that her colleague had spoken to the team leader the day before in private and they had worked out an amicable solution without the need for a public confrontation. Nevertheless, the new memes reinforce one another, they will now be even more difficult to shift.

MIMI'S STORY

But there's a problem. Her chosen course of action is totally at odds with the cultural aspirations of her employer. The company she has just joined is embarking on a new innovation programme, the aims of which are to encourage employees to challenge things, actively contribute to decision-making and bring their unique approaches and perspectives to bear. Huge amounts of time and money have been spent employing a team of external consultants to support the change programme. In order for the company to succeed in its culture change programme and for Mimi to succeed within this aspirational new culture, she clearly needs to be much more prepared to take risks and stick her neck out. The assumptions she has made will lead her to behave in a manner which is directly contrary to the future aspirations of her employer and will ultimately prove to be a far more powerful influence on her behaviour than any of the initiatives within the change programme. In order for this to change, her implicit assumptions need to be exposed, called out, challenged and reframed. Mimi, and all those making similar assumptions, need to be enabled to consciously choose a different path.

The desire to avoid the potential for public conflict had resulted in the issue being settled behind closed doors. This had directly led to Mimi having succumbed to a behaviour meme based on an incorrect assumption. Had the issue been aired at the meeting and discussed in a constructive and mature way, she would likely have had her initial assumption about the likely consequences of challenging management reframed. This could only have happened if the issue was treated with openness and a degree of skill. Instead, an undesirable behaviour meme was allowed to propagate in an uncontrolled and unpredictable way, thereby defeating the laudable aims of Mimi's employer.

3

IT'S QUIET....TOO QUIET
What does good look like?

Most people are happy to do something which until very recently was inherently one of the most dangerous things any of us could conceive of doing. We routinely crowd into sealed metal tubes which zoom through the stratosphere at close to the speed of sound. At a cruising altitude of 35,000 feet the average external temperature is -50 degrees centigrade, the air too thin for most people to breathe and all that protects us from this environment so incompatible with human life is a flimsy 3mm of metal fuselage. Thankfully, accidents are incredibly rare, and flying has become one of the safest ways to travel. I've no idea if it's true but it's regularly said that driving down to the local supermarket carries considerably greater risk than getting onto a passenger plane. In my case I can believe it because my local Sainsburys is on the other side of the Old Kent Road. A large part of the reason flying is so safe is because a culture has evolved around civil aviation where safety is absolutely paramount. This of course includes compulsory safety checks, tightly controlled procedures, training and monitoring, but these safety protocols alone are not enough. What makes flying so safe is that the rigorous safety standards are supported by what's known as a Just Culture.

Just Cultures neatly incorporate key components of wider safety cultures. At the heart of the concept is the belief that errors are caused by a combination of factors of which individuals doing the wrong thing is only one. Just Cultures provide the conditions under which people will be most likely to feel comfortable voicing their concerns, reporting incidents and admitting to their mistakes. An essential part of this is trust, trust that a when an issue is reported a proportionate and measured response will be taken, and learning will result so that safety improvements can be made. In Just Cultures, when something bad happens, the first question to be asked is not; *Who was to blame*? but *Why did that happen and how can we stop it from happening again?*

This is not to say that a Just Culture is synonymous with a no blame culture. Blame will be apportioned where it is warranted and will be backed up with consequences, but there is a clear procedure to be followed before this can happen. When something goes wrong the incident is investigated by independent experts without prejudice and the cause of the error is categorised in three distinct possible ways. The first category is the genuine honest slip, the inadvertent error. In this instance, sanction of the individual is not appropriate, to do so would ensure that people would be unwilling even to admit to the smallest innocent mistake. An appropriate response would be to provide support to the individual involved while learning as much as possible about what led to the error, so that protocols can be put in place to ensure that the same issue is much less likely to happen again. These could be procedural in nature or consist of training interventions for example.

The second category of error is the *at-risk* behaviour. This is characterised by a choice being made which, while increasing the chances of a particular outcome deemed desirable, also increases risk. In these instances, severe sanction is not initially considered appropriate, instead the perpetrator is coached in order to help them to understand how their choice of action has led to the additional risk. If this risky behaviour is repeated, the response can be escalated into the third category, namely negligence. Negligence is defined as a conscious and deliberate disregard for the rules, or a wilfully destructive act committed without consideration for the possible negative outcomes. This third category warrants sanction regardless of whether the chosen course of action resulted in negative consequences or not.

Deciding on the category of the misdeed and the appropriate sanction is often not immediately obvious, and in many cases relies on careful judgement. The primary consideration in all cases is to ensure that the incident is used as an opportunity for learning and improvement. Any sanction must be proportionate and balanced to ensure that trust is not damaged, and people are not deterred from reporting incidents. Summary dismissals in cases of negligence may at first seem appropriate and desirable, but as well as running the risk of discouraging disclosure, little learning is likely to result from such a course of action. This is particularly true when you consider that people often feel pressured to bend or break a rule when facing competing priorities imposed by leadership and that the undesirable behaviour is often a symptom of an unhealthy culture rather than the cause. This means that in many cases, care should be taken not to scapegoat individuals for wider organisational or leadership failures and more productive courses of action need to be considered.

Just Culture principles form a behaviour memeplex which provides a replicable template for effective risk management. They are principally applied in environments where the consequences of errors are likely to be severe, such as aviation, but certainly could and should be used more widely. For example, partly as a result of the response to cultural issues exposed in the Mid Staffs, in 2018 NHS England published a Just Culture Guide which was designed to '*encourage managers to treat staff involved in a patient safety incident in a consistent, constructive and fair way'*. The financial sector is another obvious candidate for the application of Just Culture principles, particularly given the fact that in the wake of the financial crisis, the main barrier to people speaking up and reporting concerns is, as we shall discuss later, the fear of an inappropriately disproportionate response. If we look at Just Culture principles relative to financial propriety rather than safety in a more general sense, the potential benefits are obvious. The adoption of these principles more widely has however been very slow to happen, largely due to an inability to get beyond the misleading platitude '*nobody can copy your culture*' and a consequent failure to recognise the transferability of key aspects of culture between organisations with very different characteristics and functions.

When we look at Just Cultures through the lens of behaviour memes, of shared assumptions driving collective behaviours, the behaviours that are indicative of a healthy safety culture are clear and obvious, and they cannot possibly rely on the assumption that everyone will do the right thing at all times. As we will see, this is a totally unrealistic expectation and fundamentally at odds with what we know about human nature. A key component of a functioning Just Culture is the prevailing assumption that accidents will always happen, so in a climate of trust it's stupid not to check, to report any concerns, have zero tolerance for anything falling short of best practice. In fact, the behaviour meme at the heart of Just Cultures is the assumption that not to do so would be a wasted learning opportunity and a dereliction of duty.

At time of writing the Metropolitan Police is coming under considerable scrutiny for its failure to address the issues raised by the report into the Daniel Morgan murder case. Following the accusation contained within the report that the Met had an *'institutional culture of corruption'*, erstwhile Chief Constable Cressida Dick issued an immediate denial. While I don't know enough about this particular case to agree or disagree with the report's conclusion, one thing is of very deep concern, Cressida Dick's kneejerk response. Circling the wagons unfortunately still seems to be a common response in these situations. This is despite all the evidence that complacency is often your biggest enemy because culture can and does turn around and bite you when you least expect it. If you don't actively look, in the knowledge and expectation that the worst can and will happen, you will eventually get bitten. As a child growing up in the seventies and eighties, I remember the media constantly feeding the public the narrative that the UK Police were the '*best in the world*', above reproach, and while corruption was a problem in other countries, it couldn't happen in the UK. I believed it at the time, but as we all now know, this was complete nonsense. It was this complacency that allowed corruption to flourish unchallenged. It was our innate preference to think the best that held sway. In the highest echelons of London's police force, it seems that it still may.

Dame Cressida Dick was also accused of blocking access to information which may have been of interest to the inquiry. Whether or not this is the case is debatable but if true, her motivation for doing so is likely to have been a desire to protect the reputation of the institution she led. The desire to protect reputations is strong. The reluctance to speak up or even confront the possibility that the organisation you lead is capable of letting bad things happen is often due to the blurring of the lines between corporate and personal reputation. The damage inflicted on the individual's reputation is somehow perceived to be intertwined with that of the organisation. This largely stems from the fallacy that senior leaders are the ones responsible for defining and exemplifying the corporate culture all by themselves. We regularly see individual leaders issuing blanket denials of the possibility of cultural problems, even when the threat to their personal reputation is small or non-existent. This is also in part driven by a desire to rally round and protect people like themselves, members of their tribe. The urge to do this is often so strong that we regularly see people who aren't personally responsible for wrongdoing go out on a limb to protect the reputation of their institutions and colleagues often at great personal risk, even when they don't have to. It also means that valuable opportunities for learning and for developing cultural awareness are not taken and that problems are likely to reoccur. People will always do the wrong thing from time to time, but the wrongdoings of the few do not define a culture, it is the reaction of the many when things go wrong that does.

Repeated annual staff surveys of Mid Staffordshire NHS Trust staff in late noughties did not indicate anything untoward. Anonymous responses to very specific questions about incidents and whistle blowing showed nothing. This is despite the fact that there must have been considerable disquiet amongst many staff about what was happening over a long period of time. When we talk about *don't ask don't tell*, we need to acknowledge that even when you do ask, given unfavourable cultural conditions, more often than not people still don't tell. The Francis report into the Mid Staffs scandal expressed dismay at how, despite array of checks and balances, such terrible experiences for patients could go undetected for so long. It's time to stop being surprised. It's time to look and look properly. However, it appears that we have learnt very little from this scandal and others like it. One of the main results of the recommendations from the Francis Report was the establishment of a network of Freedom to Speak Up Champions within every NHS Trust. This was designed to provide employees with a channel through which they could openly voice their concerns without incurring any personal risk of repercussion. A review published in 2018 by the National Guardian's Office reported only a modest number of NHS employees taking advantage of the scheme. Out of a total population of over 1.2 million employees, only 7,087 issues were reported through the Freedom to Speak Up Champions network, approximately equating to one in every 170 NHS employees within a whole calendar year. 6 NHS Trusts reported nobody using the scheme in the whole of 2017. Given these statistics, it is difficult to argue that this kind of initiative has shown much capacity to do anything to contribute to behaviour change. This should come as no surprise. The implementation of the scheme is just another example of treating the symptoms rather than the deeper cultural causes. This manifestation of the perceived need for a 'safe' channel through which concerns could be raised may actually have served to reinforce the assumption that to speak up was indeed inherently unsafe. In other words, it may have reinforced an already existing unhealthy memeplex.

In its closing submission to the Francis Inquiry West Midlands Strategic Health Authority asserted:

'...all supervisory bodies are entitled to work on the basis that the Management and Board of Trusts and the clinicians working there are persons of integrity, well qualified for their demanding jobs and carrying them out at least to a basic level of probity and competence unless and until the contrary is indicated. They are also entitled to assume that they are not being misinformed or led astray whether deliberately or through incompetence unless and until the contrary is indicated.'

Classic culture at work, shared assumptions driving collective behaviours. What this submission articulates is the belief, at least within one NHS regional body with responsibility for ensuring high standards are followed, that they are entitled to assume that everything is OK and believe whatever they're told unless and until they have evidence of wrongdoing rubbed in their nose, by which time it is too late. This questions the whole purpose and function of supervisory bodies. Their job cannot just be to wait until something obvious and indisputable lands in their lap, that cannot be anyone's definition of supervision or oversight. What this quote also highlights is the assumption that those working at the frontline are always able to make precise and accurate judgements about how ethical their own behaviour and that of their colleagues is. We know that even 'persons of integrity' can and do make poor decisions, especially when they are working in demanding jobs with competing priorities. Assuming everything will always be OK unless

IT'S QUIET...TOO QUIET

there are malign forces at work is not a reasonable assumption. These two assumptions fly in the face of what we know about what constitute strong and healthy cultures, as well as Just Culture principles.

In some environments, airlines, nuclear industry, air traffic control for example, the consequences of getting things wrong are potentially so catastrophic that any deviation from established procedures must be very carefully considered and rigorously tested before they are ever implemented. Organisations in these sectors are required to be very aware of why they do what they do and don't do. The potential downside is that these procedures have the potential become so conditioned as to become automatic and mindless. This is fine under conditions which are entirely predictable, not so when you don't know what surprise may be lurking round the next corner.

In response the money laundering scandal across its branch network in Mexico, HSBC leadership based in the Mexico City Headquarters insisted that they were unaware of what was happening. This is a very familiar refrain in common with that heard from the leadership of Credit Suisse and ING when caught up in similar scandals. They all did this while in next breath, and in reference to the widespread money laundering they facilitated, asserting something very much along the lines of; *'and besides, it's a jungle out there'*. These two perspectives do not sit happily together. If it's a jungle, you obviously need to be hyper-vigilant. Nobody without an intimate knowledge of the environment goes into a jungle armed solely with flip flops, a thong and a bottle of Evian. You need to expect that things can and will go wrong. People not bringing issues to your attention is not a sign that everything is OK, it's probably sign that you should be very worried. It seems to me *'It's quiet...too quiet'* is the responsible perspective to take. Not to be paralysed by paranoia, but to be vigilant and to refuse to take the lack of evidence of anything untoward as reassuring. It's impossible to know its precise motives for doing so for sure, but the fact that very soon after this scandal came to light, HSBC divested itself of many of its businesses in central America. In all instances, the overwhelming response from all the scandal hit banks has been to tighten procedures and processes rather than on addressing the mindsets and behaviours which had caused the problems in the first place. In other words, to again focus on managing the symptoms rather than the cause. This begs the questions to what extent the banks had acknowledged the impact of culture or how it works. It also begs the question as to what precisely were the lessons that had been learned from these failures.

Whatever forces are at work that cause people to prefer to believe that no news is good news, the important thing to acknowledge is that this extremely common tendency inevitably leads to complacency. The problem with complacency is it removes issues from focus, taking them off the agenda and reducing the amount of scrutiny that people place on their decisions and their actions. It also means that vital opportunities for learning are missed. For this reason, complacency is almost always a key factor in cultural failures. It is also one of the biggest barriers to the development of cultural self-awareness.

In healthy risk cultures there is no room for complacency and need for vigilance is not the sole preserve of risk and compliance functions or oversight bodies. It is a function that everyone must perform, not merely those with a professional responsibility for oversight. One of the major benefits of a Just Culture is that it very effectively counters this shifting of responsibility. In the Francis Report, this phenomenon was blamed in large part for a failure in lapses in the standards of care from being called out. The assumption that someone else will take care of problems leads to a lack of personal action, particularly from non-medical staff who are inclined to defer to the medical experts. When someone thinks, *"that's not my job"* with respect to issue reporting, they are really thinking, *"Someone else will do it, so I don't need to."* When everyone believes that someone else will do it, the result is that nobody does it. In this case, shared assumptions driving collective inaction. This phenomenon, often described as the bystander effect, is greatly strengthened when even the smallest amount of personal risk is associated with the act of speaking up. It is also enhanced when you believe that there are people better placed than yourself to step in. A common tactic for fighting the bystander effect is to call people out individually for a response, in irrespective of their role or expertise. Removing risk and instilling a culture across all roles that says '*this is your responsibility*' ensures that everyone can be held to account. Having ownership of culture residing with a few leaders or 'expert practitioners' obviously has the potential to stifle this outcome.

Culture is immersive and all-pervasive. It is the water in which we swim, the sauce in which we are marinated. The notion that it can be directly determined and controlled from on high by senior leadership is unrealistic. Think of the starling in the flock. By far the biggest influence on its behaviour comes from that of its immediate neighbours. This means that what is required to change culture is the direct participation of everyone. What then of the role of leadership in the process of change?

While their influence and ability to define culture is usually greatly overestimated, leaders are likely to have greater influence than any other single individual within an organisation. This is often termed '*setting the tone from the top*' as when looking for cues as to how to behave, many will of course look to their leaders for a behavioural example. This is never truer than when they are looking to justify their own questionable behaviour. Just as we are able to define healthy cultures, are we able to define what effective leadership looks like with regard to culture beyond the obvious role modelling of desirable behaviours?

COUNTING THE DANCE STEPS

In 1978, James McGregor Burns contrasted two distinct leadership styles. transformational and transactional. Transformational leadership does what it says on the tin in that it is a process that facilitates changes in individual and collective behaviour. When at its most effective, transformational leadership builds motivation, morale, and performance through encouraging followers to identify with the collective organisation, its values and goals. Transformational leaders may inspire others through role modelling, but they also challenge them to be autonomous and to assume accountability for their work, while helping them to understand their strengths and weaknesses. They are characterised as exhibiting leadership traits such as open-mindedness, empathy, and humility. By contrast, transactional leadership is based on give and take, where emphasis is on supervision and oversight and the main levers of influence are sanction and reward. A key part of Burns' distinction was that transformational leaders strive to facilitate culture change, whereas transactional leaders operate within the prevailing culture without attempting to change it. Transformational leaders can be found at any level within an organisational hierarchy, not just within the boardroom, and they may not even have any formal management or leadership responsibility. In transformational leadership, what Burns describes is the ability to create the conditions under which organisational change can happen.

In essence, transformational leaders exert their influence without the need for procedures and processes to help them. They inspire people to take responsibility for their own actions with their personality and vision as well as their behavioural example. This strikes me as a great way of conceptualising the difference between leadership in its purest form, and management. Managers need to be provided with the procedural levers for change, such as performance management processes, disciplinary and reward systems in order to influence behaviour, true leaders do not. While distinct, transformational and transactional leadership styles are not mutually exclusive. There is nothing to preclude a transformational leader from using sanction and reward to affect behaviour, these are just additional tools in their armoury which can complement their innate influencing skills. Transactional leaders of course have a far more limited tool kit to draw on.

The problem here is of course that the biggest day to day influence exerted on the vast majority of employees in all but the smallest organisations, comes from local leadership. These leaders are often nothing of the sort, according to the definition above, they are almost exclusively managers. Personal charisma is not something you will often see on competency frameworks and is rarely an explicit requirement for management positions. Instead, our managers are required to be apparatchiks, and we traditionally provide them with a whole range of procedures, process, and tools to encourage them to be so. Even at the highest levels within most organisations truly transformational and charismatic leaders are exceptional and very far from the rule. Against this backdrop, how realistic is it to expect our management to lead culture change without considerable additional support? Culture change driven through by dint of the pure qualities exhibited by charismatic leaders remains, for most organisations, purely aspirational. This means that for an organisation attempting to use leadership communications as the main driver of change, the reality for most is that their initiatives will be doomed to failure. We need to be much more realistic about the extent to which local leadership is truly capable of articulating a compelling vision for change. In most instances, this is an extremely difficult task, a fact that many of the widely used change management models fail to take account of. Whilst we do need to expend time and energy articulating the case for the need for change and vision, we have to be realistic about how much this can actually achieve on their own.

There is however an important and often overlooked facet of transformational leadership that potentially holds the key. It is not reliant on some innate and largely unteachable skill of personal charisma. It is effectively empowering others to act. Transformational leadership is of course precisely just that, transformational, and much of the power to drive change resides in a leader's ability to pull everyone into the process through active inclusion and involvement. This, as we know is a key determinant of success in any culture change process.

The problem is that any act that could be perceived as effectively handing over the reins of control to those without management responsibility is of course deeply counter-cultural in many organisations. Doing so can pose a significant challenge to many leaders and managers, both in terms of the way they see their roles, as well as the traits and skills they need to do it successfully. For managers reliant on transactional levers of influence, creating the local conditions under which culture change can happen involves going well out of their comfort zones. To support the process of change and minimise the amount of discomfort experienced by managers, organisations can do two important things, firstly, to provide them with a clear process to follow, and secondly to equip them with the skills they need to implement the process effectively.

In most organisational contexts what is expected, valued, and rewarded in leadership roles still adheres to a very traditional and stereotypical template, and mostly involves '*leading from the front*'. Various research studies conducted by Conflux have consistently shown that traits such as competitiveness, decisiveness, confidence, and assertiveness are still perceived to be valued and rewarded in leadership far more than traits like empathy, open-mindedness, compassion, and collaboration. This perception holds across all employee groups from organisations in a range of sectors. It is however, not the traditional transactional 'power' traits that yield results when seeking to drive change, it is the transformational, interpersonal traits that really matter.

As part of an investigation into the cultural underpinnings of the gender pay gap in the NHS, Conflux conducted a research study of 6,000 employees in 2018. It assessed the extent to which people from a number of Trusts across saw a range of different leadership traits being valued and rewarded in talent management decisions, such as promotions and recruitment into leadership roles. Across all employee groups there was a consistent belief that transactional traits such as confidence, assertiveness, decisiveness, and competitiveness were valued and rewarded most. By contrast, transformational traits such as empathy, compassion and open-mindedness were rated as being significantly less important. While this is not an unusual finding, it fails to reflect one of the core values of the NHS.

> *'We ensure that compassion is central to the care we provide and respond with humanity and kindness to each person's pain, distress, anxiety or need. We search for the things we can do, however small, to give comfort and relieve suffering. We find time for patients, their families and carers, as well as those we work alongside. We do not wait to be asked, because we care.'*
>
> NHS core value statement

No respondent group believed that the core value of compassion was being given a high priority in their Trust's talent management decisions. There was however a very different profile when they were asked to rank the traits that they believed should be valued and rewarded in leadership if their Trust was to perform at the highest possible level. Empathy, open mindedness, and compassion were rated as the most desirable traits and competitiveness ranked least desirable of all traits. Decisiveness and confidence continued to feature near the top, reassuring in a healthcare setting where handwringing and indecision are certainly not to be encouraged, but still well below empathy and compassion. This finding showed that the core value of compassion was reflected in the way people believed things should be, but not in the way they believed things actually were. The striking thing was that this was a consistent finding across all employee groups from all trusts regardless of role, seniority, or personal demographics. This shows how communicating core values and gaining buy-in from staff is not enough to define or change culture. Despite a clear and strong consensus to the contrary, a behavioural preference for traditional transactional leadership continued to hold sway. This seeming paradox is resolved when we analyse it in terms of behaviour memes.

The shared assumption about what is valued and rewarded is what drives the collective behaviour, not a belief in an ideal, no matter how universal this belief may be. Against the prevailing assumption about what is valued, if I want to be successful when putting myself forward for a senior position, it makes much more sense to place emphasis on how confident, decisive and competitive I am than to emphasise my compassionate, empathic side. Conversely, if I'm a decision-maker, the least risky option would surely be to reflect the perceived prevailing organisational norm by selecting or promoting on the basis of the same traits. In short, it is the perception of the way things are that reinforces culture through behavioural responses, irrespective of a widely shared belief in how different things should be. This situation is allowed to persist because the prevalence of these behaviours means that individuals remain unaware of the fact that their views about the ideal are almost universal. A classic self-reinforcing feedback loop. Increasing collective awareness of the existing consensus it is a first necessary step in disrupting this loop, thereby increasing the chances of change.

The results to the assessment conducted in the NHS of what leadership traits are valued show that culture is often very different from the sum of its parts. They also show that it is the perceived reality that drives behaviour, not the desired end state, however wide the consensus. This means that even if we have complete agreement across an organisation as to what is the ideal target cultural state, this may still not be enough to change people's behaviour. Consider this in light of the fact that most culture change programmes focus on aligning people, with communications and training as the main focus. The intention behind this is to galvanise a consensus for change. This is a fundamental stage in the vast majority of commonly used change management models despite the fact that alone, it cannot drive change. If shared assumptions drive collective behaviours, you must change both the behaviours and the observed consequences of these behaviours in tandem. It is only then that we will break the cycles of self-reinforcement to enable change. In the case of the NHS and many other organisations we assess, is the assumption that transactional and non-inclusive leadership traits are most valued actually true? Yes, but only because this assumption reinforces the behaviours that make it true.

Another great example of this kind of circular reasoning affectively reinforcing stereotypical views of leadership is when the ideal profile of an effective leader becomes self-defining. Senior leaders are, by definition, successful within their own cultural environments, and they can readily become the template that defines what good leadership looks like. The nuance that gets lost in this kind of reasoning is the fact that senior leaders have reached the boardroom through an ability to succeed within their current organisational culture, not because they exemplify any universal characteristics that define able and successful leadership in any generalised sense. In a different cultural context, they may not have succeeded to anything like the same extent. In many instances the outcome of conforming to a narrow, traditional definition of what leaders should look like results in homogenous leadership teams, very often predominantly white and male. This kind of self-reinforcing cycle can exert a profound influence on behaviours in a way that can be very difficult to break free from, even if there is a collective acceptance of the need for change.

This research also highlights the extent to which humility remains an under-valued quality in leadership. This is not just because of collective traditional stereotypes but also in the minds of individual employees. Humility is consistently neither seen as being valued, nor desirable in leadership across all sectors Conflux has investigated. This is despite the fact that humility is a key attribute of a transformational leaders and humble leaders are extremely effective at building healthy cultures. This is something acknowledged by Burns in his definition of transformational leadership as well as many others. Humble leaders are more approachable and open to challenge, honest about their mistakes and shortcomings and as a result, more forgiving of those of others. This also makes them authentic and trustworthy. Their lack of personal competitiveness makes them more likely to acknowledge good work and the strengths of others, which motivates employees to share ideas try new approaches. Humble leadership allows for the creation of diverse, multidisciplinary teams displaying a range of abilities and perspectives in an inclusive environment where innovation can flourish.

Cultivating humility as a leader requires knowing when to ask for help and giving credit where it is due. Being comfortable admitting that you don't know everything demonstrates a willingness to grow and acquire new skills and knowledge, and an openness to new ideas and a desire to reach common consensus regarding shared goals and responsibilities. In short, humble leaders create the conditions under which a healthy culture can thrive. Despite this, humility is consistently seen as both one of the least valued and valuable traits in leaders. This is likely to be down to the fact that humility is commonly viewed a weakness, incompatible with power traits such as confidence, decisiveness and assertiveness. This is far from the truth. It takes a strong and confident leader to admit their shortcomings and present an honest and unvarnished version of themselves to everyone. What's more, the need for humility actually increases as the leader's duties and responsibilities increase in scope. But the higher up the corporate ladder a leader climbs, the harder it can be for them to remain authentic and humble. Career success can lead to over-confidence in some. In others, increased levels of self-doubt regarding the ability to function at the highest level can lead to defensiveness and perceived arrogance.

When we have such a demonstrably effective templates that can be applied to major aspects of organisational culture such as Just Culture and transformational leadership, why is it then that we're constantly fed the line that organisational cultures are unique and cannot be replicated? The usual platitude that's trotted out is *'anyone can copy your business strategy, but nobody can copy your culture'*. Sure, culture cannot be lifted wholesale and transplanted into another organisation, but there are clear best practices that can be learned from and shared, and leadership traits and abilities that can be nurtured and selected for. In the absence of an awareness of underlying assumptions, behaviour memes come into existence in organisations without regard to business objectives and reproduce within the context of the prevailing culture, regardless of how healthy or unhealthy that culture may be. Healthy cultures can be defined as those that provide for the basic physical and psychological needs of their members, reinforcing positive assumptions and desirable behaviours. Unhealthy cultures can be defined as those that create the behaviour memes that inhibit the outcomes compatible with long term success. They induce and reinforce behaviours motivated by fear, that cause people to be excluded, that fail to provide a shared sense of values and purpose and that stifle innovation. Unfortunately, in our current workplaces, when we define them in this way, healthy cultures appear to be the exception rather than the norm.

Another word which is constantly used in connection with culture in an unhelpfully imprecise and lazy way is 'strong'. What exactly do we mean when we say *'strong culture'*? In researching for this book, I came across a change consultancy website which gave the example of people wearing what they like at work as a sign of a 'weak' culture. Others cited things like free breakfasts, walking meetings, concierge services and duvet days as constituent parts of a 'strong' culture. Let's be clear, these are all artifacts and may even be the paper over some pretty serious cultural cracks. The ability of a culture to function well in the absence of such artifacts is a sure sign of a strong culture. What defines a strong culture is not piecemeal hacks, but the extent to which collective behaviours are guided by shared values.

There has rightly been considerable focus on core values as a means of defining guiding principles by which everyone should adhere to and thereby shape culture, but the efforts to imbue these has been patchy at best. There should be no considerations higher than core values, but unfortunately in many organisations, they are subsumed by competing priorities when it's expedient to do so, in order to achieve immediate goals. Another reason core values can often be circumvented is when they come up against dogma. In recent years this has been exemplified by social media providers who have allowed core values such as *'don't do evil'* to become overridden by a dogmatic adherence to the belief that the internet should remain totally independent and democratic, free from excessive regulation. This has been allowed to happen despite the emergence of increasingly compelling evidence, some of it gathered by the firms themselves, of the damage an unregulated online environment can cause to some of the most vulnerable people in society.

Culture is often described as organisational DNA. It's not, core values are, or at least should be. Values should be largely immutable, the permanent bedrock upon which everything should depend. Strategy will change based on external conditions and demands and therefore so should culture. What's required is agility, a constant fine-tuning to realign culture in response to these changes. If you have a culture that fails to align to your strategic objectives, your organisation can die a slow death. If you have a culture that fails to align with your values, it can die a quick one. Whichever happens, the ultimate result will be the same.

Culture, values and strategy are often confused and conflated. We need to be clear about what they are and how they are different. Here's another analogy, imagine a ship at anchor. The ship is the organisation, the anchor is values, the

IT'S QUIET...TOO QUIET

weather, tides, waves, and wind are the external conditions demanding changes in strategy. The anchor chain is the culture. The culture forms the connection between core values and the strategy. There must be flex or the boat will be pulled under by tides and waves, but not so much that the boat drifts too far from its values.

Flexibility and adaptability are desirable traits, but always within certain parameters. Staying true to core values needs to be what ultimately governs the decisions that people within organisations make. These are fixed and immutable and give organisations resilience and stability. The trick is to flex around these core principles. Just like in any natural system that is governed by fundamental laws there is room for accommodation, but it is not a free for all. Not allowing people the leeway to exercise discretion in their work risks driving a wedge between organisational and their personal values. This is demotivating and destroys a sense of meaningfulness. Values cannot be imposed on people externally, so we need to find a way to allow people to find the connection between their personal values and those of the organisation. This requires thought, discussion, and exploration. It also requires making values explicit through exemplar behaviours and from a memetic perspective, articulating the specific assumptions that drive them. If we impose values-based rules on people, we must find a way of doing so without taking away their autonomy and discretion. The values that drive high-performance cultures are not those which inhibit the use of discretion, they facilitate it through open communications and feedback, allowing people to take considered risks to innovate for example. We should not attempt to tell them what to do in each and every context, instead we should help them to develop and use the skills which will lead them to the right course of action in a range of circumstances, however unexpected many of these may be.

Unfortunately, the reality is that most organisations attempt to inculcate core values through communicating values statements which are typically anodyne, entirely predictable and utterly forgettable. The good ones are relatively few in number so tend to stand out. Twenty years ago, I was involved in assessing the impact of the new values programme at Channel 4 Television. Unlike almost every other values programme I have been involved with before or since I can still remember what the values statements were. They were *'Inspire change'*, *'Make trouble'* and *'Do it first'*. Clearly, to me at least, they were memorable, but why? They were certainly unusual, but what also made a real difference was that they pointed directly to the desired culture in explicit behavioural terms. They were behavioural exhortations that laid down a challenge to employees as they were actually very hard to enact successfully. What's more they are helpfully vague, making people curious and prompting discussion about what they meant and how they could be lived up to.

When organisations embark on a values programme much of the effort and resources are dedicated to communication. But communicating values is never enough in itself, and the process certainly cannot be didactic and unidirectional. Even the simplest and most ubiquitous values such as *'Integrity'* and *'Customer focus'* fail to convey to people what they mean in terms of expected behaviours. Internal Communications functions are usually owners of the process of rolling out values programmes and naturally see this as a short-term communications challenge and an initiative rather than an ongoing endeavour. Even when employees can tell you precisely what the values statements are, values driven actions are still not always clear and obvious. In many cases, having a set of core values statements plastered on every office wall, actually inhibits meaningful discussion about what the right course of action might be under a range of different circumstances. Allowing core values to be subsumed by other priorities certainly can be a step on the road to ruin but allowing them to exist as mere slogans on a training centre wall is unfortunately all too common. Failure to ensure that everyone is involved in an ongoing dialogue about what they mean in terms of behaviours can and often does, lead to disaster.

IT'S QUIET...TOO QUIET

While strong cultures are those firmly rooted in core values, they also need to exhibit the capacity for flexibility to accommodate inevitable change. Organisations need a culture capable of supporting an appropriate range of responses to different types of problems. If a highly controlled bank's reaction to damaging misdemeanours is to respond with further controlling measures, as they do all the time, this is likely to exacerbate the problem by further reinforcing the culture that allowed bad practice to flourish in the first place. This has been the actual response of many institutions to the financial crash. They have tried to enforce a compliance culture that further strips individuals of the requirement to use their moral judgement, creating an environment where challenge is even less tolerated than before. Results-orientated individuals or those heavily incentivised to achieve results will always be tempted to find a work around. This is especially true for people within an ultra-controlling, rules-based culture, where they feel compelled to look for means of finding loopholes or otherwise circumventing the strict rules that govern their actions. Unfortunately, our financial institutions tend to be both massively controlling while at the same time providing huge individual financial incentives for short-term results, the classic double whammy.

In response, our financial institutions have quite rightly looked to core values for help. I do not know of a single one that does not list integrity, or a synonym of it as a core value. While this is on the face of it reassuring, culture has gleefully stuck a spanner in the works. The top-down paternalistic nature of these organisations means that there is an assumption that everyone knows what the right thing to do is. You tell people what to do and they do it right? Wrong. What the right values-driven course of action is, is very often far from obvious or clear cut, especially in the real world of competing priorities. Reaching a consensus on what the values-driven course of action is must be arrived at through careful exploration and discussion. In other words, integrity cannot be prescribed. Unfortunately, it requires the kind of discourse that our more traditional institutions are unused to indulging in. Having integrity as a core value in such circumstances can easily reinforce unhealthy complacency.

As mentioned earlier, it is not the actions of the few to cause things to go wrong that defines culture, it is the reaction of the many when they do. What really makes the difference if suspected bad practice is uncovered is the extent to which an organisation encourages discussion and challenge around what is right and wrong. These are the conditions under which the right course of action will be identified early to allow potential bad practice to be nipped in the bud. Sometimes there just is no obvious 'right' thing to do. In these circumstances the best you can be expected to do is do show a level of thought that allows you to justify your choice of response, based on careful consideration of guiding core values. This requires ongoing evaluation of potential courses of action and their likely implications. Risk and compliance functions should not see their role as to simply lay down the law. External oversight bodies are of little use if they can only act when things have already obviously gone astray. An important part of the job of these bodies do must be to proactively work to inspire the discussions and evaluations which have a chance of preventing such problems in the first place.

Critically evaluating the ethical considerations around different potential courses of action is habitual. It is a competence that will improve with practice. It should not be the preserve of leadership, specialist functions or oversight bodies, everyone should do it. There should not be an automatic requirement for teams to defer to leadership when confronted with a moral or ethical dilemma, and the conversation that needs to take place is in essence a very straightforward one and certainly doesn't need to be facilitated by consultants. It consists of *'what do you think we should do/should have done'* and *'why?'*. The next step is to enable a group to implement their decisions as they believe is best. Empowerment is a horrible 'consulty' sort of word, but I can't think of a better one.

IT'S QUIET...TOO QUIET

In complex organisations with a range of specialist functions and skills requirements, division of labour should not result in compartmentalisation of responsibility for what's really important. This means that shared values need to be augmented by a shared sense of purpose. In the bank, even until relatively recently the message that percolated down from leadership was that the purpose of the organisation was to create value for its shareholders. I heard this sentiment expressed many times even by those with 'responsibility' for organisational culture. Personally, I found this assertion very far from a rallying cry in terms of motivating me to come to work every day and expend discretionary effort, and I'm sure I wouldn't have been alone in this. More importantly, whichever way you look at it, the ultimate purpose of any organisation is to provide a product or a service to customers, service users, patients and wider society. They are the ones that ultimately pay the bills, salaries and dividends. In terms of a commercially focused organisation, it is their ability to serve customers effectively and efficiently that will determine their financial success. This allows them to make a profit and create shareholder value, it is certainly not the other way around. Nevertheless, it is all too common for leaders to see their purpose as a self-serving one, with their ultimate job being to protect the interests of the organisation they lead. This is in many ways natural and understandable but losing sight of a higher purpose and a wider perspective inevitably leads to problems.

Days or even weeks would pass in my part of the bank without one ever hearing the word 'customer' being uttered. This was largely because at the top of the termite mound we were very far removed from the coalface of the branch network and call centres where interaction with customers happened. This is not uncommon as many company functions and senior management are primarily focused day to day on strategy, products or sales, and customer centricity can easily be considered a priority only for those directly involved in providing a service to customers. Of course, providing superior customer service makes sense in all sorts of ways for a business, including the fact that it is the most effective means of creating a shared sense of purpose. Customer centricity means putting customers' best interests at the heart of everything you do. This includes understanding their needs and preferences, and knowing when we are falling short, in other words, exhibiting empathy and humility. But unfortunately, as we will know, these are traits that are hugely undervalued within many organisations.

In his book Service Fanatics, Dr James Merlino describes how one healthcare provider, the Cleveland Clinic, transformed itself from a hospital focused purely on technical excellence to a patient-centred organisation based on empathy. The key to this was uniting all the employees behind a shared purpose of providing an excellent standard of patient care regardless of whether they are doctors, receptionists, hospital porters or caterers in the canteen. Successful implementation of the transformation programme required that everyone, regardless of role, was held accountable for providing excellent standards of patient care, either directly or indirectly. Within this new culture, there was no room for separate behavioural standards between any groups, whether they were medical or support staff. A major part of the transformation involved recognising everyone as a caregiver with a responsibility to provide the highest standards of care and to voice any concerns they might have about their own, or their colleagues' ability to do so, at the earliest opportunity. It is easy to see the benefits of this kind of shared focus within a healthcare setting, perhaps a little less so in more commercially focused organisations, but it's hard to argue that they would not also benefit from it.

Our collective inability to get to grips with organisational culture has consequences for us all. It is no exaggeration to say that failures in organisational culture have claimed thousands of lives and even more livelihoods. And yet we are capable of getting things right. We know the cultural attributes of socially responsible and high-performing organisations that act with integrity and probity. We have concrete examples of best practice which can be learned from and

IT'S QUIET...TOO QUIET

replicated if only we had half a mind to do so, and there is no more important time than now to start. Just Cultures are examples that exhibit a fundamental quality required for the creation of a healthy risk culture, but to what extent can we identify defining characteristics of healthy cultures more generally? To help understand what these qualities might be it is useful to consider how cultures came into existence and what culture is for. What is the purpose of culture? This may seem like an odd question, but nothing as universal and powerful as culture comes into existence by accident.

COUNTING THE DANCE STEPS

4

THERE'S A WOLF IN MY KITCHEN
What is culture for?

There's a wolf in my kitchen. I call him Ned. At the moment, he is curled up in his favourite chair fast asleep. Wolves and dogs belong to the same species, Canis Lupus, with dogs being categorised as belonging to the subspecies Canis Lupus Familiaris. Dogs and wolves share more than 99 percent of their DNA. Ned could in theory successfully procreate with a she-wolf, although looking at him now would suggest that neither party would have much of an appetite for it, albeit for very different reasons. Every morning I take Ned up to the park at the top of the hill where he plays with the other wolves. There's Ethel, who's about the size of a small rabbit and looks a little like a gremlin, Belle, who weighs about the same as me and looks a somewhat like a yak, invisible under a profusion of black and white hair, with every size and shape in between.

It has been estimated that as long as 40,000 years ago, dogs began to diverge from wolves and over the last 1,000 years or so they have been selectively bred to create the huge variety of breeds we see today. Like humans, wolves are social animals, they are also extremely adaptable and have been able to colonise an incredibly varied range of environments. It was this ability to modify behaviour that led some of them to start their long association with mankind, and the evolution of dogs came about as a direct result of close contact with humans. Wolves were initially drawn to human settlements as they provided a great place for scavenging for food. It was the least timid wolves who benefitted most from this bounty and passed this trait and its commensurate benefits down to their offspring. This was the start of the domestication process that over many generations resulted in the development of the intimate relationship between dogs and humans we see today.

Ned spends most of his time in the company of humans however, and like many generations of his ancestors has never met a wild wolf, yet in many respects his behaviour remains extremely wolf-like. He likes to roll in smelly things, he buries bones, he wags his tail when he's happy, his tail droops when he's sad or fearful, he spins around before settling down to sleep and he feels compelled to mark his territory on just about every tree he comes across. These are all behaviours characteristic of wild wolves and have persisted in Ned, all of his chums in the park, and his compatriots found in every park across the world. This is despite the fact that virtually none of them has ever met a wild wolf.

In rare circumstances the usual roles of dog and human have been reversed, with very consistent and predictable results. In 1991 a young girl was found in a kennel in Ukraine where she had lived in the company of dogs for over six years. She had moved in with the dogs after having been neglected and ignored by her alcoholic parents. By the time she was discovered she had almost entirely modelled her behaviour on her canine guardians rather than on her human parents, including walking on all fours, growling and barking. This grim story mirrors similar ones across the ages, some of which remain rooted in folklore, others of which have been rigorously authenticated, studied and documented. In each case, the pattern has been the same with the children adopting the behavioural characteristics of their animal surrogates. The good news was that in the case of the young Ukrainian girl, the behavioural patterns were reversible, allowing her to eventually resume a relatively normal 'human' life.

While these stories involve two of the most social and adaptable animals on the planet, the differences between the reactions of each species to being raised in one another's company is stark. While the wolf's or dog's capacity to modify its behaviour in response to its environment is considerable, the human capacity to do the same is clearly infinitely greater. This is because humans are much less driven by innate instinct. When we are born, we are in many ways behavioural blank slates. The behaviours that make us human are acquired through experience and imitation rather than having their origins in genetics. It is the fact that we have become largely untethered from the behavioural constraints of instinct that has allowed us the behavioural flexibility to be able to adapt and thrive in so many different environmental contexts. Imagine a circumstance where a child was to be raised without any external human influence of any kind. Other than in their physical appearance to what extent would they be likely to be identifiably human? Almost certainly in very few behavioural respects. Humans are unique in their capacity to adapt their behaviour in response to different environments and it is this that lies at the heart of our ability to form distinct cultures. In fact, it has been argued that the creation of culture is a defining characteristic of humanity. It also means that under certain circumstances, we all have the capacity to do things that under 'normal' conditions we would never countenance.

Nothing as universal and powerful as the human capacity for culture comes about by accident. It is an ability that has the power to convey on individuals and the groups they comprise the possibility of numerous competitive advantages. This capacity itself is to an extent benign in that it can equally result in successful and unsuccessful outcomes depending upon the cultural attributes that are exhibited relative to the external environment. Nevertheless, there are certain characteristics which are common to all successful cultures. The most obvious of these is the fulfilment of the need for safety and belonging, the most basic of human needs. It was the young girl's neglectful parents' inability to fulfil this need that drove her to seek the company of the dogs.

Other individual and group needs that culture can help to satisfy are a shared sense of identity, values, and purpose. These help to build cohesion by defining what characterises the group to which you belong as distinct from other tribes. The ability to work as part of a cohesive group conveys practical benefits such as an enhanced ability to solve complex problems through shared, cumulative learning, innovation, and the division of labour. The inherent benefit of these characteristics is apparent in organisational cultures just as much as societal ones. When we look at culture in this way, to say that we do not know what good looks like in terms of culture is absurd. The shared assumptions that define healthy work cultures are that they are safe and inclusive, driven by shared core values and purpose where new ideas and innovation can thrive. The collective behaviours that these assumptions engender, create a virtuous feedback loop that mitigates against all kinds of negative outcomes. These include corporate scandals caused by moral or ethical lapses, ineffective risk management and inequities based on gender, ethnicity, or disability.

5

EVERYBODY DANCE!
How can we build an Inclusive Culture?

Engendering a sense of safety and belonging is perhaps the most important objective when attempting to build a healthy organisational culture. As well as the obvious and pressing moral imperative of providing diverse and equitable workplaces, we also know that inclusion is an absolute prerequisite for an engaging culture where employees are the source of innovation and effective front-line risk management. Despite this, we have made virtually no progress in our ability to measure and improve the inclusiveness of corporate culture in the last 20 years.

Our progress in diversity, equity and inclusion has been depressingly slow and most of our corporate boardrooms are still predominantly inhabited by white men. The majority of our companies have significant disparities in pay between men and women and between white and black and ethnic minority employees. There is an increasing recognition from our business leaders that this is something that needs to change. A common response from them is to make pledges to increase the proportion of women and people of colour at senior levels. This is relatively straightforward to achieve and the effectiveness of this is kind of response is readily measurable in terms of bums on boardroom seats. It also entirely misses the most important point. It is the very definition of treating the symptom rather than the cause as gender and racial imbalance is an artefact with the root cause residing in deeper culture. Simply to triage people into senior roles based on their demographic profile without addressing the underlying causes of inequality can at best be only a temporary fix. Analysis by the Office for National Statistics found that around two-thirds of the UK Gender Pay Gap (GPG) is due to factors other than age, working patterns or location meaning that most of the disparity is caused by 'unexplained' factors. These factors are cultural, and despite increased focus on talent management processes and diversity metrics, the GPG has remained broadly static for the last 15 years. A collective failure to address organisational culture is at the heart of this lack of progress.

In 2000, the Coca Cola Company agreed to pay $192.5 million to settle a race-discrimination lawsuit, at the time the largest settlement of its type in U.S. legal history. Coke also agreed to implement comprehensive changes to its talent management practices including hiring, promotion, and reward, promising to become what it termed the "gold standard" of fairness and equal opportunities. The company was also mandated to make changes to its procedures and practices, with their response monitored by an external task force of experts appointed by the lawyers of the plaintiffs to help ensure compliance to the company's efforts for the next four years. These were to cost an additional $36 million on top of the original settlement. Coca Cola's efforts to promote greater diversity soon broadened to encompass all racial minority groups and female employees. The task force's work which was originally scheduled to end in 2005, was extended by incoming CEO, E. Neville Isdell, a man with a strong track record championing racial equality. The company began monitoring best practices by applying data analysis to all elements of its talent management processes to identify disparities in recruitment, pay, bonus or promotion decisions. All talent decisions were scrutinised for fairness. A requirement for all job slates to be diverse was introduced, with at least one female or ethnic minority candidate required for each opportunity. Senior executives were incentivised through their pay structure to increase diversity within the divisions they had responsibility for. In short, Coca Cola threw the kitchen sink at it.

By 2010, these considerable efforts appeared to be an unqualified success with black employees holding 15% of senior leadership roles compared to a mere 1.5% in 1998. In annual employee surveys, employees' perceptions of fairness at Coke increased steadily year on year and by 2007, Coke was ranked fourth on the Diversity Inc. Magazine's list of top 50 US companies for diversity. Fast forward to 2020 and these dramatic changes had largely been reversed. Turnover amongst black employees had soared, and a restructuring in 2017 had resulted in an effective closing off of the pipeline of black talent into senior positions. The proportion of black executives had almost halved to 8% and the overall percentage of black employees fell to 15%, 5 percentage points lower than it had been in 2000.

What could have caused this dramatic turnaround? Coca Cola's own assessment, as well as that of many others, has been that following the initial successes, a sense of complacency had begun to set in across the company. There may be some truth in this assessment and as we know, complacency is often the biggest barrier to change but, in this case, how could we explain the rapid loss of many of the hard-won gains? Surely if Coca Cola had just taken its foot off the pedal, there would have been a halt to progress rather than such a precipitous decline. They had done all the right things according to change management orthodoxy. They had articulated a clear and compelling business case for change, there was real commitment at the highest levels, a huge amount of time and resource had been dedicated, improvements were incentivised across leadership and an external oversight body had been set up. All the change management boxes had been ticked and yet the majority of the progress had failed to stick. The reason for this was that their focus on diversity and metrics had failed to address the true root cause of their problem, namely the absence of an inclusive culture. Their dependence on changing processes and procedures meant that they were focusing on artifacts and like many before and since, all their efforts were directed at treating the symptoms. They had failed to expose and address the underlying assumptions which had created the problem in the first place. Old mindsets and behaviours had temporarily had their impacts mitigated by the enormous efforts of the company but were quick to re-emerge when priorities shifted. In 2021, Coca Cola pledged to re-establish addressing inequality as a key priority with a programme aimed at improving its hiring and promotion practices with regard to black employees at all levels. It seems that even after their experience of the last 20 years, Coca Cola unfortunately may have learned little about what really drives lasting change.

This problem is not confined to the US. Since the recently introduced a legal requirement for all employers of over 250 people in the UK to publicly disclose their gender pay gap data, it has become clear that many employers don't have a clue about where to act to close the gap, beyond treating the symptoms through target setting and diversity monitoring. In her accompanying statement to their 2019 gender pay gap report which showed a 50% pay gap in favour of men, slightly more than the previous year, the Group Director of Human Resources of HSBC issued a plea for help in addressing the issue.

> *'We welcome input and ideas, either on the content of this report or on our wider diversity and inclusion strategy'*
>
> Elaine Arden 2020

This is a refreshingly open approach from an organisation like HSBC. While stopping short of saying *'help, we haven't really got a clue about how to deal with this'*, it was acknowledgement that with all the internal and external resources and expertise at their disposal, they were still in need of fresh ideas. One can only speculate about what will happen if, or more probably when, organisations are required to report on their ethnicity pay gaps.

The requirement to publish GPG data has laid bare the extent of the problem of gender inequality in the UK, but despite published figures showing an average disparity of 18% in the UK in favour of men, 72% of men and 68% of women surveyed by Conflux in 2019 still believed that people succeed on merit within their organisations. The percentages rise to 93% for male, and 83% for female senior managers. This effectively means the very people most empowered to initiate and resource improvement actions are the most complacent, and least likely to acknowledge that there is a problem. The figures also show that it can be difficult for people to consider the objective evidence in acknowledging the extent of the issue. The fact that culture exerts its powerful influence in subtle ways and operates largely at an unconscious level means that obvious disparities between perception and reality are able to persist.

If we accept, as we certainly should, that the ability of women and black and minority ethnic employees to fulfil leadership roles is no less than that of white males, we have to accept that most companies are falling short of providing an environment where anyone can succeed on merit. Leaders have obvious difficulty in acknowledging the extent to which their companies are falling short with regard to meritocracy. In most cases, they have succeeded within the prevailing culture, so to question the meritocratic nature of their businesses is to question their very legitimacy as leaders. You will never hear a CEO saying 'We have a black woman heading up one of our European Divisions, given the glass ceiling we have constructed here, chances are she'd probably be much better than me at my job'. Conversely, we regularly hear business leaders who have successfully convinced themselves of the meritocratic nature of their companies, emphasising how they beat the odds by rising through the corporate ranks despite coming from humble, unprivileged origins. In a truly meritocratic culture, there would be no odds to beat, their success would be entirely unremarkable and not worthy of drawing attention to, and yet many still feel compelled to do so.

These contradictions clearly show the gulf between espoused values and objective reality. This mismatch is not only misleading, but positively damaging. MIT Sloan School of Management professor, Emilio Castilla has described this disparity as 'the paradox of meritocracy'. This describes how a belief in the meritocratic nature of their business leads decision-makers to also believe that their decisions are more impartial than they really are. This allows people to unconsciously act on their own biases, believing they are in fact being impartial, and as a result fail to scrutinise their decisions or actions. In short, the belief in the meritocratic nature of the company leads directly to increased bias, thereby decreasing overall meritocracy. Another clear example of a behaviour meme, assumptions driving behaviours in a mutually reinforcing way.

Early in 2021 the Financial Times published its second 'Diversity Leaders' list. These are the companies most highly rated by their employees in terms of their belief that their organisations are meritocratic and promoted diversity. This was measured through attitudinal questions rated on the dreaded 5-point Likert scale using statements such as *'I believe my employer provides an environment where anyone can succeed on merit'*. The list largely consisted of organisations which, like the vast majority of their peers, remain beset by pay gaps and the under-representation of women and minority groups at senior levels. This kind of research, while being almost ubiquitous, tells us nothing about the relative state of inclusion in these companies. What it does highlight however is the single biggest barrier to progress, complacency. Against the almost universal corporate backdrop of inequality and unfairness, employees telling us that everything is fine is the worst possible starting point for driving change. The true 'Diversity Leaders' are organisations that encourage their employees to constantly challenge their practices and build self-awareness that allows them to acknowledge both individual and institutional biases. The list also shows us after 25 years of conducting research into employee experience and culture, how little progress we have made in asking the right questions, interpreting the responses correctly and using the insights to enable positive change.

Instead of taking such misleading research at face value, despite how reassuring it might initially seem, we should be constantly self-critical and vigilant. Over the years, through the use of employee surveys, we have become so conditioned to see responses that are favourable, that is those that reflect the organisation in a positive light, as inherently 'good'. If we want to create change to build more inclusive cultures, what we should be doing is to challenge complacency, and where required unquestioning positivity to drive down the percentage of people who still believe everything is OK. In few other areas is there such a gulf between what organisations value and espouse and how they behave. On almost every corporate website you will see pompous and self-congratulatory statements regarding commitment to Diversity & Inclusion and fostering a culture where everyone can thrive irrespective of gender, ethnicity, disability, or sexual orientation. Most clearly don't and in most cases, a more accurate characterisation should be *'we abide by the law and try not to deliberately discriminate against anyone'*. In fact, as we will see, this is the question that many people seem to be answering in their heads when they complete an employee survey asking them if they believe their organisations are fair and meritocratic. This is after all the most efficient way of resolving cognitive dissonance and protecting leaders' self-images as champions of diversity, equity, and inclusion. While racial and gender inequality and pay gaps are priorities to be tackled with urgency, they are symptoms of a much deeper fundamental cultural malaise. They indicate a more generalised tendency to exclude people who fail to fit a predetermined and narrow template that defines what a 'successful' employee should look like. Before we explore this in greater detail, it is useful and instructive to define some terms.

EVERYBODY DANCE!

Let us start by drawing a clear distinction between diversity, equity and inclusion as they are concepts which are often confused or conflated. Diversity is about demography, the population numbers. Equity is about fairness, the fair distribution of power, money, and influence, which may not be equal due to the need to recognise that people from different backgrounds are coming from very different starting points. Inclusion is about behaviours and assumptions, the culture. Diversity is relatively easy to measure, it's about populations and percentages. Equality is also straightforward to measure in most cases, although equity less so as it requires a value/legal judgement about what is fair and unfair. Organisations have a reasonably good record of tracking diversity and equality metrics. For example, the standardised method for gender pay gap reporting in the UK is based on a very simple calculation. There has been much debate over whether this calculation is over-simplified but nevertheless this has provided a consistent means by which employers can quantify, compare and track one particular equality metric. In most cases they can relatively easily use employee records to get an overview of the proportion and distribution of minority groups across the organisation.

Inclusion is related to diversity and equality, but distinct. As the Coca Cola example clearly shows, you can hire diverse talent, promote employees from under-represented groups to senior positions, and even change pay structures to help ensure pay equality and incentivise progress. But all these efforts are mere window dressing and unsustainable if you do not have a culture of inclusion. An inclusive culture will help to ensure that your diverse talent can be successful and will be motivated to stay with you. This means that sustainable diversity and equity are in fact direct outcomes of an inclusive workplace culture, which acts as the bedrock of all your efforts.

Despite being the engine for diversity, equality and equity, inclusion very rarely gets effectively measured or proactively managed. Much has been made of the business benefits concomitant with diverse and inclusive workplaces, and these are indisputable. Wider inclusion is about valuing difference in all its forms and is not just about discrete issues such as gender, race or sexual orientation. This is because the individual differences within the different gender, race and ethnicity categorisations are far greater than the differences between them. These differences encompass individual skillsets, personality, thinking and problem-solving styles and neurodiversity for example. Of course, having a diverse employee population that reflects that of your customer base in terms of protected characteristics allows an organisation to anticipate and respond to the needs of all of its customers better, but it is the wider differences that provide the diversity of thought that convey most other important benefits to organisations. An exclusive focus on the most salient differences between groups such as race or gender, however well-intentioned, can limit our efforts to build inclusive workplaces in this wider sense. This is quite simply because in the absence of overt discrimination, the behaviours that support an inclusive workplace are the same whether you are black, white, male, female, gay or straight. Looking at difference in its broadest sense possible, maximises the benefits that valuing the full range of possible difference brings to a business. Despite this, many businesses remain exclusively focused on the undoubtedly important, but somewhat more myopic task of ensuring that there is no downside morally, legally or reputationally with regard to race, gender, sexual orientation and disability.

Inclusive cultures are most often defined as ones where difference in all its myriad forms is valued. Valuing difference allows a range of perspectives and ideas to be heard and actively considered. This in turn enhances innovation and improves the quality of decision making. Homogeneity within teams can certainly limit the scope of group discussions and impoverish their quality, but the benefits of diversity can only be realised if the group is operating within an inclusive environment. Research consistently shows that the greater the variety of opinions expressed in group discussions the greater the effort group members expend in order to explain and defend their viewpoints. This greatly improves the quality of discussion and the chances that different possible courses of action will be properly scrutinised and evaluated. In this way, they are more resistant to common causes of bias such as groupthink or confirmation bias. Inclusive workplaces also engender a feeling of belonging and psychological safety for all employees. As mentioned previously, this has huge benefits in terms of the commensurate behaviours that people exhibit. Risk management processes are greatly enhanced by people's increased tendency to question things they may be uncomfortable with, conduct open discussions around what does and doesn't constitute values-driven behaviour, to admit to their mistakes and call out those of others. Innovation and creative problem solving can only thrive in an environment where people feel comfortable articulating new ideas without fear of judgement or ridicule, and where they are given the chance to take considered risks in implementing them without negative consequences if they fail. Inclusive workplaces are self-reinforcing in that they attract, develop, and retain a diverse range of talent. And while inclusion is not a panacea, it is the single most important prerequisite for many of the characteristics that define a healthy culture, helping to avoid the common pitfalls that can damage an organisation's performance or reputation.

We rightly focus on demographics such as gender, ethnicity, disability, and sexual orientation when investigating differences in opportunity and experience between different groups, but the concept of inclusion goes much further than this. While it is of the utmost importance that inequities and discrimination are tackled in the workplace, it is not an absence of these that defines an inclusive culture. The tendency for D&I professionals in HR departments across the world to focus all their attention on instances of unfairness with piecemeal interventions, while in many instances entirely necessary and understandable, limits our ability to further our understanding of how to build inclusive cultures in the widest possible sense. Worse still it can serve to reinforce the view that many unenlightened leaders unfortunately still have, that diversity, equity and inclusion (DEI) is a peripheral issue just affecting 'minority' groups. The unfortunate truth is that many DEI professionals are still unfairly seen by some as conducting self-referential and arcane discussions, unrelated to the successful running of a business.

In his book of the same name, William Deresiewicz describes generations of students emerging into the world of work from America's most prestigious academic institutions as *'Excellent Sheep'*. In the book he castigates top tier US universities for failing in their duty to provide a fully rounded education where students are taught how to think rather than what to think. One result of this is to create a talent pipeline to management consultancies and the boardrooms of the future that is generic and myopic in terms of diversity of thought. This is despite the fact that this elite student population is increasingly both better balanced in terms of gender, and drawn from diverse backgrounds, nationalities and ethnicities. Deresiewicz argues that instead of business focused degrees, these universities would be better offering elite students liberal arts degrees which provide a broader platform for developing a comprehensive range of skills and perspectives. The extent to which educational institutions do or don't contribute to the lack of diversity in corporate boardrooms is open to debate, but as we have seen, across different types of employees in very different organisations, the assumed preferred profile of what leadership looks like remains narrow and stereotypical. In response some employers have consciously begun recruiting from a wider range of educational institutions than ever before, but to a large extent the excellent sheep are still destined to become excellent tadpoles.

So, how do we start measuring the inclusivity of a workplace? To do so, we need to define what inclusivity looks like in visible and quantifiable terms and what does it feels like to be part of a truly inclusive group culture. The observable characteristics of an inclusive group that distinguish it from those of a less inclusive group are not merely the fact that people are treated with fairness and respect. This is important, but it is a hygiene factor. Without fairness and respectful treatment for all, a group's performance will certainly suffer, but achieving it will only bring performance up to a baseline level and no higher. So, what is it about an inclusive culture that brings real business benefits? The answer to this question is incredibly simple. Inclusive workplaces are characterised by desirable behaviour, with people doing the right things for the right reasons. These include actively contributing to discussions, asking questions, making suggestions, and taking accountability for following them up, challenging the status quo and taking considered risks to innovate. All these behaviours are measurable and quantifiable. These are usually considered the beneficial outcomes of building a healthy culture, but in fact they are not dependent upon culture, they are the culture.

If leaders are to play a role in helping to nurture an inclusive team culture, does an inclusive leader actually do that less inclusive leaders don't? The answer is they create the conditions under which people feel able and encouraged to exhibit these beneficial behaviours as well as instilling a belief that team members will benefit from doing so. In order for this type of environment to be established, core traits such as empathy, open-mindedness and humility are crucial in team leaders. For example, it's not winning an argument or exercising control over the group that matters, it's reaching the right decision. The quality of decision making is enhanced when a range of viewpoints are expressed, listened to and actively considered and these interpersonal traits are essential for this to happen. Unfortunately, these are traits that are not often nurtured in the workplace, even less valued in leadership. As we have seen, it is traits such as confidence, assertiveness and competitiveness which continue to be widely seen as being most valued in leadership. Most organisations continue to demonstrate that they operate with a very narrow definition of what effective or appropriate leadership looks like. This definition is very often grounded in traditional stereotypes and there is very little opportunity for those who fall outside of these restricted parameters. This results in homogeneous and imbalanced leadership teams not only in terms of demographics, but in a much wider sense.

One group which is consistently overlooked and under-represented at senior levels are introverts. Social confidence and an outgoing personality are often conflated with leadership ability, and consequently rewarded with greater opportunity and management responsibility. There is no known association between performance in the vast majority of roles and the personality dimension of introversion-extraversion, and yet we repeatedly see quiet achievers not having enough of a voice and being side-lined for development and promotion. In practice an overly confident and assertive manager can actually have an extremely inhibitory impact upon a working group that stifles many of the culturally advantageous behaviours we are looking for team members to exhibit.

Rather than take comfort from the automatic assumption that they are inclusive and meritocratic, or address issues through crude target setting, companies would be well-advised to ask themselves some deeper questions. Are the people who enjoy the greatest success within your culture those who can, or at very least appear to operate with complete authenticity because they fit in by dint of who they are? Do our talent management processes and reward structures reinforce stereotypical views of leadership that inhibit the maintenance of diversity and equity? Are leaders simply products of the prevailing culture and strong maintainers of the status-quo, and if so, to what extent will change actually be difficult or impossible? What percentage of your leadership team are tadpoles who have only ever worked for one company? To what extent do you exhibit a collective growth mindset where there is sponsorship and encouragement for all employees demonstrating a capacity to learn and grow, without a focus on small number of high-flyers resulting in a self-fulfilling prophesy? Can anyone really succeed on merit without their future being dependent on past achievements and academic background rather than on potential? These are the kinds of questions that very few organisations routinely ask themselves but are ones that, when answered objectively, would expose many uncomfortable truths.

Some years ago, I applied for a job at a large well-known global consulting firm by mistake. For the purposes of this story, I shall call this firm Balding & White. I was made aware of the post through an employment agency who had made direct contact with me with a phone call out of the blue. They were unable to tell me much about the role other than it was to work with clients on 'improving their corporate cultures'. Despite this scant job description, they assured me that I struck them as a very good fit for the role. In all truth at the time, I had only limited knowledge or experience in the area of culture, but I thought it might be worth learning more about the opportunity. I agreed to let them put my name forward.

I was interviewed by a severe and immaculately turned-out man of military bearing who I imagined to be just a few years older than myself. He commenced the interview process by telling me all about their new and important initiative with enormous growth and revenue generation potential. They had an illustration to prove it. It was a black and white line drawing of three pillars supporting a triangular roof. It was a picture which exuded classical authority, intellectual solidity, and permanence. It was clearly pictorial equivalent of a model and had been dreamt up within a few months of the financial crash to exploit the growing concern clients were expressing over the financial and reputational threats unmanaged cultures were increasingly being shown to pose. The Culture Pillar was one of three new service lines which constituted their High-Performance Portico. To make this absolutely clear, the left-hand pillar had *'CULTURE'* written on it in Roman font and the roof was labelled *'HIGH PERFORMANCE'*. The role I had applied for was to lead the Culture service line and they were also recruiting leaders for the other two pillars. I can't remember what was written on the other two pillars, but he clearly saw himself as the roof.

I asked him about his background and what had led him to this area of work. He explained that until recently he had worked as a tax accountant, but that he had always harboured an interest in culture. He talked of his 'career trajectory' and that this was an 'exciting' and 'natural' next step for him. I asked him what his career up to now had taught him about corporate culture. He proceeded to tell me at some length how he had learned from all the diverse people he had interacted with in various contexts over his career as a tax accountant. It was becoming increasingly obvious that neither B&W nor this role were for me, but I thought it easiest just to continue going through the motions. I could feel myself tuning out. I imagined in my mind's eye, half a lifetime of interactions talking about tax accounting with tax accountants from tax accounting teams from financial institutions specialising in tax accounting. I imagined what a the typical 'trajectory' looked like from the launchpad of a solid middle-class upbringing and probable expensive private education, leading to an upper second-class honours degree from a reputable Russell Group University straight into an accounting firm and management consulting. The problem with a trajectory is that a rapid rise and a levelling off is always followed by an inexorable and accelerating decline. Why would you swap a nice safe and presumably lucrative career in tax accounting in a tax accounting firm for the far riskier endeavour of heading up an entirely new service line in an area you had no previous experience in?

Then I suddenly realised that he had stopped talking and was looking at me with eyebrows raised expectantly. Could he have asked me a question and was awaiting a reply? I could have asked him to repeat what he'd just said, but I didn't. This was partly because of the risk that he hadn't actually asked me a question, but mostly because of a concern that he might simply just dive back into detailing his interactions with all those tax accountants. One thing I had learnt from these kinds of not too uncommon situations where I found myself not listening to what was being said, was to simply come straight back with a question of my own. It's a tactic my family are very familiar with.

'How would you describe the culture here at Balding and White?' He looked a little surprised.

'That's actually a really good question' he muttered. He paused to collect his thoughts. 'How would I describe the culture here at B&W?...Yes, umm…that is a good question.'

The hesitation and the vagueness in the way in which he answered the question made me ask myself whether he had given the issue much thought before. It seemed that this culture thing might be something that applied only to clients willing to part with money for their services, not B&W itself. He alluded to the OCI, a well-known culture assessment tool;

'Passive aggressive'. He'd obviously read a book.

'Have you applied the OCI here at B&W?' The answer was 'No'. I don't remember a great deal about the rest of the interview.

Of course, I didn't get the job. From the scant feedback I later received the main reason for being rejected was, rather ironically, not being the right cultural fit for B&W. They were probably right of course, but nonetheless I wondered what had led them to this conclusion. What did it actually mean? Were they telling me I wasn't passive aggressive enough? Or perhaps I was too passive aggressive and didn't fit in with some aspiration to change their culture in future. I concluded that it was probably just a simple case of just not fitting some unspecified anticipated profile of a Balding & White employee. Ironic, given that I am both white and balding.

Anything is better than pretending you are selecting on the basis of cultural fit when you have made no attempt to define what your culture is, or what your future culture needs to look like. All this does is to provide you with an easy way to justify deeply biased decisions. The obvious and much better alternative is to select on core values. At least these have a chance of being reasonably well-defined and supported by illustrative behaviours which are more amenable to assessment during an interview. If they had knocked me back on the basis that I hadn't shown adherence to their core values of courtesy and integrity it would have stung, but at least it would have made some kind of sense. After all I hadn't really shown him the courtesy of listening to what he was saying and was clearly more than happy to make stuff up.

According to their website, one of Balding & White's core values was a commitment to diversity and inclusion, full as it was with statements about how it valued different perspectives and approaches as much as women and minority groups. All very laudable, but actually very tough to live up to. Selection on the basis of cultural fit should not mean *'excluding people who don't think and act like us'* but unfortunately in many cases it seems to. They may as well have just told me that we don't want you because your face just doesn't fit.

Imagine for a moment that Balding & White lived up to its core value of inclusion in its hiring practices. This would mean selecting for fit within the current culture would be completely incompatible with the requirement to value different perspectives. If you need to select on the basis of something, don't do it on some vague notion of cultural fit, do it on the basis of fit with values and do it properly. Be clear on values being assessed and what the criteria for selection or non-selection are in terms of concrete attitudes and behaviours. To assess candidates based on undefined ad-hoc subjective criteria flew in the face of their actual espoused values and would in all likelihood, perpetuate an unhealthy monoculture.

In addition to their fledgling Performance Portico, Balding & White had a specialist Talent Practice which advised clients on recruitment amongst other things and a Diversity Practice which did the same for diversity and Inclusion. Definitely a case of physician, heal thyself. Everything's relative I suppose as in my experience to get any kind of feedback at all could actually be considered good practice for other professional services consultancies. At about the same time I accidentally applied for a similar role at one of B&W's equally well-known competitors and also famous for their talent management and DEI practices. I still haven't heard whether I got the job or not, but the interview was 13 years ago, so I guess it's safe to assume that I didn't.

All qualified HR practitioners know what best practices in talent management look like. They form some of the most basic guidelines that define how organisations manage recruiting, career advancement and promotion with fairness and consistency. The problem is these guidelines are very often not followed. The example from Coca Cola Corp shows that while they may not actually have the power to create inclusive cultures, rigorous talent management processes certainly increase diversity and equity. It is only when present in conjunction with a culture of inclusion, that this hard-earned diversity will be sustainable along with the business benefits commensurate with it.

Applying a structure to key talent decisions is widely recognised as helping to reduce errors by ensuring that decisions are made intentionally, based on evidence and consistent judgement criteria. When there's effectively no structure or oversight of decision-making, people end up making decisions based on assumptions or gut feelings that reflect unconscious biases. Despite this, less than half of employees surveyed by Conflux report that they see their organisation using structured processes for meetings, interviews or evaluations. When organisations don't have structured processes, or people fail to follow them, they greatly increase the risk of biased outcomes. This is never truer than for employers whose confidence in their ability to make objective unbiassed decisions causes them to fall foul of damaging complacency. It seems that the very organisations claiming to specialise in talent management may, by definition, be more likely than others to be exemplars for the paradox of meritocracy.

6

WELCOME TO THE TERMITE MOUND
Symbols and rituals

Termite mounds tower up to 9 metres above the ground. While externally they are relatively plain and featureless, internally they are complex and sophisticated structures full of tunnels, galleries and chambers. The tunnels extend underground to allow for safe entry and exit for the termites and radiate in all directions to enable foraging and the collection of food. In the centre of the mound, running up its entire height, is a large internal airspace called a chimney, which provides access to the network of tunnels within the mound. The mound is more than a nest, it can be considered the external body of a superorganism made up of thousands of individual workers, soldiers and the queen. The individual is nothing. The entire purpose of termites is to dedicate their lives to the benefit of the wider colony.

It was my first morning at the bank. Of course, I had been there before throughout the rather protracted interview process, but today was different. I looked at everything through new eyes. I was now officially one of them.

Despite being over 3 miles away I could, and still can, see the tower from my living room window. It is one of a cluster that comprise London's main financial business district. My journey to work was a straightforward one and required only one change on the tube. The main staff entrance to the tower was directly accessible from the tube station via an underground mall. This meant that with the exception of the 200-metre walk from my house to my nearest tube station, the entire journey to work could be made underground. If I got bored of the canteen or the food served at the tower's many cafes, I could instead spend lunchtime 'foraging' for food in the subterranean mall. This meant that unless I made a concerted effort to do otherwise, the entire working day could be spent without going above ground outside.

From the mall employees could take a short escalator ride into the ground floor atrium. This was awe-inspiringly huge, similar in scale to most cathedrals and was patrolled by a large number of security guards. At the centre of the atrium was the tower's core which contained the lifts which transported the thousands of employees to and from their individual workstations within the tower's labyrinthine internal structure.

I was now clearly working in a termite mound- with lifts. I was now part of the super-organism, something far bigger and more powerful than myself. Just like a cathedral, the atrium spoke to me, not in a yell but in a still small voice. Only this place whispered '*If you toe the line, you'll be nurtured and protected, after all you're one of us now. If you don't, you'll be crushed like a bug.*'

Symbols are assumptions made concrete. They reinforce culture in a way that exerts a collective influence on behaviour. The symbolic power of this new work environment certainly exerted a strong influence on me as soon as I entered it, and I can only imagine this was also true for my fellow new recruits. This feeling only persisted for a short while, after which it just became just plain normal. It was not until I'd left, did I truly understand how profound this impact really was.

A few years ago, I visited Lloyds Banking Group head office in London to discuss a potential culture assessment focusing on Diversity and Inclusion with a senior member of the HR team. The main entrance where I was met led straight to the lifts and after a short ascent, we entered a long corridor along which were portraits of all the company chairmen through the ages. These were hung in strict chronological order so as we walked along the corridor, the elaborate moustaches and mutton chops of the Victorian era gradually gave way to the clean-shaven look of today's modern executive. Despite the obvious historical differences there was a striking similarity between each portrait. In each case the subject had a slightly stern bearing with a steadfast look of dependability. The most obvious thing was that they were all white and all male. As we walked along the corridor, my host caught my eye and was obviously thinking the same as me given the context of our meeting. '*Yes, I know*' she said, and with a shrug *'but what can you do?'*

History is undoubtedly important to culture, but so is symbolism. Symbols are concretised assumptions, and while they do not have the power to create or change culture, they do much to reinforce it. One could not help but imagine how the sequence would continue in future. In 50 or 100-years' time, would we still be looking at a continuous line of similarly countenanced middle aged white men? Maybe yes maybe no, but still this gallery did much to reinforce the view that this is what leadership is supposed to look like. These portraits were hung in the main thoroughfare that led to the meeting rooms which were in constant use. If the portraits had been hung elsewhere, somewhere say more akin to a corporate museum rather than a busy functioning part of a modern building, the effect on the viewer would be very different. They would most likely be seen as Lloyds' corporate cultural past, rather than its present and probable future.

7

TURNING TADPOLES INTO FROGS
How do we create a learning culture?

Learning and innovation in organisations is often described as being analogous to the evolutionary process. There are certainly parallels but there is one very important distinction. Genetic evolution is made possible by rare random mutations which may or may not confer a species with a benefit in terms of their ability to survive and thrive within their particular ecological niche. Those that are beneficial will, by definition proliferate, those that don't will disappear. The whole process is entirely without purpose or motive and is driven by blind luck. Organisations are also shaped by a process of replication, not through genes, but through memes, which determine the collective behaviours of the people within them. But unlike animal species, corporations can make conscious self-directed changes in response to current or anticipated changes to their business environment. They have the potential for self-determination that animal and plant species have never had. Those that adapt to external change will survive and those that don't will go to the wall. Yet when we look at the corporate 'fossil record' we find it looks very much like the evolutionary fossil record in that it is littered with extinct forms. These include once thriving organisations such as Kodak, Xerox or Sears. This shows how even the most successful can and do find the process of self-directed change and adaptation difficult to achieve and then even more difficult to sustain, even when their own very existence is at stake. For such extinct giants, the inability to proactively manage their cultures meant they, like those species preserved in the fossil record, were also at the mercy of random forces that determined their fate.

In the case of Kodak, the inability to innovate is usually cited as the cause of its demise. While this may have been a part of the reason, it only tells half of the story. Its insistence on continuing to focus on film and film cameras while the rest of the world was moving to digital photography ultimately led to its downfall, but this was despite Kodak having actually developed the first digital camera. It was not an inability to innovate, but an unwillingness to risk investing in this new format that created the problem. This example clearly shows that the capacity for innovation alone is not enough. It is the ability to accompany this with a willingness to take a risk and implement innovative solutions that really matters. Kodak had the key to its future success in its hands and let it go. It did so because of an unwillingness to adapt its core business to a potential new reality. It suffered from a circular logic that said *'we provide people with film because that is what they are buying'* only to find that when they were provided with an alternative, their customers moved on very quickly and left Kodak behind. They failed because while they demonstrably had the capacity to produce innovative products, they were unwilling to be truly innovative for fear of disrupting their own market. This was because the company had failed to accurately define its core purpose, which was to provide its customers with the most effective means of capturing and recording significant images and events through the medium of photography, not to make and sell film.

Just as with organisational change, there are two main drivers of biological evolution. The first is change in the external environment. The second important driver is isolation. A population that is isolated from the rest of its species for any length of time will almost certainly develop in a divergent way from the parent group. The impact of both these conditions on the speed of the evolutionary process illustrates what is known as punctuated equilibrium. Equilibrium in an evolutionary sense is a condition where a gene pool is in stasis because evolutionary forces are in balance due to stable external environmental conditions. In ecosystems this tends to be the norm for long periods of time. In genetic terms, for hundreds of thousands of years we see little evolution because ecosystems are in a balanced, unchanging state. From time to time, events occur to disturb this equilibrium which then requires genetic changes within species to adapt to the new normal or die out, this is the condition called punctuated equilibrium. An obvious example of this type of force were the climatic changes created from the meteorite that wiped out most of the dinosaurs and heralded the rise to dominance of mammals and birds.

What, if any, implications could this have for modern organisations? The increasing pace of change now means that the evolutionary drivers of cultural change are constant rather than intermittent. For this reason, you don't have to dig far to find the fossils of once thriving tech companies. This is the sector where change is most rapid, so the need for learning and innovation is therefore the most pressing, and the lack thereof has the most immediate consequences. In today's business landscape, punctuated equilibrium has become something more akin to continuous disequilibrium. This disequilibrium is often caused by newcomers into an established market with new products or services. We call these newcomers disruptors for a good reason. If we adhere to the prevailing view that culture change is necessarily slow and painful, against a business background of constant change, who is going to invest in tech in the expectation of anything other than purely short-term gains? In an environment of continuous disequilibrium, organisations must exhibit the capacity for rapid and ongoing adjustment if they are to survive.

What we also see exhibited within organisations is that isolation does indeed drive innovation, mirroring one of the major forces driving the evolution of species. Innovation is something that tends to happen not at a macro level or within formal R&D functions, but within individual groups across an organisation that are isolated from the forces that tend to impose conformity and rigidity. This is precisely what happened in the case of Kodak. The first digital camera indeed developed in isolation from the company's core research and development activity, but unfortunately for Kodak, as a result, investing in its development was not made a strategic priority.

To extend the genetic analogy, we know that a small gene pool caused by low genetic diversity greatly reduces the ability of a species to respond to environmental changes thereby increasing the likelihood of extinction. In the same way, the meme pool of an organisation consists of all the memes within the employee population. The culture is therefore determined by all the assumptions and corresponding behavioural responses contained within it. A large and diverse meme pool is analogous to a large gene pool in that it will contain the capacity for a greater range of potential responses to change, meaning that the chances of successful adaptation and survival are greatly enhanced. If we consider excellent sheep or high-flying tadpoles, it is clear to see how organisations may unwittingly be reducing their capacity for innovation, adaptation and therefore their chances of long-term survival.

When assessing individual potential and the ability to respond to inevitable future change, current knowledge is less relevant than the capacity to learn. Having a particular perspective or knowing the answer to a question is clearly less important than having a capacity to reach a viewpoint through critical evaluation and logical reasoning. This largely depends on having the ability and willingness to be curious, maintain an open mind, to challenge the prevailing orthodoxy and ask the right questions. A work environment where employees are supported to think independently and demonstrate effective learning behaviours is increasingly referred to as a learning culture, or innovation culture. Most of the learning that happens within organisations does nothing to develop the employees' future learning capabilities and behaviours. Instead, the bulk of learning tends to fall into two broad categories. Firstly, there is learning for compliance, which places the greatest value on inculcation of the rules and procedures required to fulfil statutory legal requirements. We have all been subjected to online sheep dip compliance training, a primary purpose of which is to indemnify the organisation from legal action when things go wrong. The second is job-specific training, designed to teach employees the specific skills and processes that are necessary purely for successful current job performance. This usually happens during induction or upon the implementation of new processes or technology. Both these types of learning exemplify those very forces that tend to impose conformity and rigidity. An excessive focus on these types of learning stifles innovation and the development of a true learning culture as they stress the importance of what to think and do rather than how to think. The same is true for didactic values training which fails to focus on the development of critical evaluation skills in regard what constitutes values-driven behaviours. Continuous learning is something that becomes an integral part of everyone's day to day work. This is usually in informal contexts, so may not be seen as learning and certainly not as training.

Double loop learning as first described by Chris Argyris in the 1980's has since become a widely applied concept in organisational learning and development. It describes the process by which people develop the ability to deeply analyse their own assumptions and beliefs at the same time as learning in more traditional contexts. Double loop learning is a core competency in transformational leadership, as it allows deeply held assumptions to be examined and potentially reframed. It is therefore critical to the process of understanding how culture impacts upon the individual and group behaviours. This is because this kind of learning can only happen when underlying assumptions which have largely been taken for granted, and have therefore remained unchallenged, are brought to the surface into the individual and collective consciousness. An example of this process in action would be the establishment of an interactive dialogue between members of a group, which allows its members to identify and question potentially unhelpful assumptions that drive undesirable behaviours which act as barriers to change or run counter to organisational values or aspirational cultural state. The starting point for this type of dialogue has to be the examination of objective evidence for the existence and nature of these underlying assumptions in a clear and readily comprehensible form. This is why effective assessment is an essential core component of any well-designed culture change process. Discussion of the assessment outputs provides the ideal starting point for this, and the discussions should therefore be on building cultural self-awareness within the group. This counters the kind of behavioural myopia we see in many organisational contexts that inhibits self-directed adaptation and innovation. The process should provide a simple method for examining and understanding what would under other circumstances be seen as too every day or ordinary to be considered worthy of this level of discussion. This encourages participants to start thinking about the self-imposed limitations the individuals and group may have unconsciously constructed around how they behave and think as well as identifying self-reinforcing behaviour memes. In essence this means helping our tadpoles metamorphose into frogs.

While on the face of it there may appear to be opposing forces at work, maintaining a balance between single and double loop learning can only be mutually beneficial to both. There is for example an understandable desire for compliance, coherence and adherence to common goals and values. There are also considerable social forces which influence individual behaviour when they are part of a group that encourages conformity that can lead people to do things they would normally not countenance. Pitted against these is the need for individual difference, new ideas and ways of thinking, challenge and innovation, in other words, maintaining a large and diverse meme pool. Whilst these may at first sight seem incompatible and mutually exclusive, they do not have to be. A balance can be struck in treating organisational core values as guiding principles that require regular discussion, while at the same time exploring what they mean for behaviours in various contexts, rather than as written in tablets of stone.

The key to building an innovation culture lies in nurturing curiosity and learning skills and behaviours in your employees, rather than relying purely on formal learning and development programs. Constant reinforcement of positive behaviour memes around risk taking, accountability, open feedback and challenge will do more to build a stronger learning culture than any formal training possibly could. Rewarding these behaviours alone is not enough, the creation of a work climate where they are nurtured and expected without a fear of creating discord or tension is also essential. In an environment where innovation and challenge is welcomed, a degree of conflict is inevitable. Conflict is often seen as a sign of an unhealthy working culture, but it is the collective inability to manage conflict that is the issue, not conflict itself. No group of people will agree about everything all the time and conflict happens when people care and feel able to express their opinions openly. A team where no conflict ever arises is actually an indicator of an unhealthy culture where apathy rules or overbearing leadership stifles open dialogue. This is increasingly referred to as a *'culture of toxic niceness'*, but this term can be extremely misleading. Niceness is never toxic when it is genuine and based on empathy, especially when it comes from leadership. Only when motivated by fear or an excessive desire to avoid any potential conflict does it exert a negative influence. For this reason, a key part of the learning programme must include strategies for dealing effectively with potential conflict within the group.

In contrast to the formalised learning that helps people to build work-related skills, continuous learning in an innovation culture becomes something that encourages people to naturally exhibit the behaviours that allow learning to happen. It is not something that is formally required of them or that they do in a conscious or deliberate way. These behaviours are simple and natural. For example, people are born naturally curious, they ask questions, construct and test hypotheses, experiment with different ways of doing things but unfortunately these are behaviours that many of us gradually unlearn as we get older. Curiosity and open mindedness are key traits that allow learning to happen but are often significantly undervalued in work contexts. They may even be actively discouraged. Rewarding curiosity does not just mean recognising those who demonstrate a willingness to involve themselves in self-initiated learning, it's also about creating a climate that nurtures critical thinking, where challenging authority and speaking up are encouraged, even if this risks creating some degree of conflict. This is particularly important if you want your team to produce something innovative and have the courage to implement it.

The absence of a true learning culture is characterised by a failure of the organisation to learn about itself. This may either be because of a reluctance to do so or a failure to appreciate the importance of this kind of learning. When cultural failures happen, it is often within organisations who display a reluctance or inability to ask the kind of questions of themselves that risk exposing difficult truths or challenging comfortable self-perceptions. The desire to protect reputations and to project a positive corporate image inevitably has profound impacts at all levels of the organisational hierarchy. At a time when most organisations expend considerable time and resources in managing their corporate brand reputations, where virtues or strengths are trumpeted and shortcomings glossed over or rationalised away, it is easy to forget the value of learning from mistakes or negative feedback from customers, employees or wider society. This has fostered a mindset that has led us to the ridiculous situation where we actively incentivise our employees to tell us through formal feedback mechanisms that everything is fine and that nothing needs to change and react with complacent self-congratulation when they do. It is however impossible to change anything when you are unaware of the need for change or unjustifiably complacent about your current behaviour.

In the course of my work over the last 20 years I have spoken with many organisational leaders about the importance of building inclusive learning cultures and the possible mechanisms that can be utilised to help to make this happen. One thing I have learned is that the idea of giving employees more of a voice, encouraging challenge and increased decision-making latitude over their work and how they do it can be extremely threatening to more transactional leaders. A very common objection I hear is that they don't believe that they are culturally 'ready for it' as an organisation. This kind of circular reasoning obviously makes any kind of culture change all but impossible as by definition never doing anything counter-cultural will never result in any change. But to be fair to them, what I believe they are really saying does not relate to culture, they are actually expressing a doubt that their people have the skills needed to support these kinds of outcomes. This concern is one that is often well-founded. There will always be a qualitative element to all the behaviours which define a healthy work culture and the skills that define them are often not given sufficient attention. Being able to personally contribute to a culture where the desirable behaviours are encouraged is best seen as a competence which can be nurtured and developed, not just in leaders, but more generally. Giving direct and open feedback is a skill, as is receiving it. Speaking up in a challenging but constructive way is a skill. Responding to being challenged is a skill. Articulating a new idea is a skill. Listening to and considering new ideas in a non-judgemental way is a skill. Decision making is a skill. Cultural awareness is also a skill. All of these can be developed and nurtured and are needed to complement the behavioural changes commensurate with a healthy work culture. It is beyond the scope of this book to go into detail about building skills in each of these areas, but I would like to explore one overarching skillset that influences all the others, giving and receiving open feedback.

Despite the fact that one of the best ways to improve employees' performance is to tell them what they are doing wrong, managers often prefer to avoid these difficult conversations, so they end up providing more positive than negative feedback. The truth is that people often fail to recognise when their behaviour fails to match cultural expectations, especially when they are not very self-aware, so feedback is critical to helping them to start doing the right things. Of course, feedback that is less than positive must be provided constructively and tactfully and this is an important skill for any people manager. What gets much less recognition however is the important skill of receiving open feedback and using it to learn and grow. Feedback is not just top-down information sharing from management or formalised performance management discussions. Neither is it solely about sharing negative information. Difficult conversations through structured performance reviews can of course be necessary components of feedback, but they should only be a small part of the picture. Feedback is actually about colleagues of all types actively contributing, generating ideas for innovation, providing recognition for one another's achievements and offering constructive input on areas for possible improvement. This should form an ongoing dialogue that happens daily and is fundamental to an inclusive team culture. If feedback happens only under exceptional circumstances or at specific times such as the annual performance review or when somebody's made a mistake, it cannot become an integral part of the team culture. It must become part of business as usual.

Feedback is a powerful tool to increase performance as when handled with skill it builds self-awareness, trust and the capacity for innovation. It offers opportunities for recognition and creates learning opportunities for all to build on strengths and encourage continuous improvement. Ideally feedback should be seen, wherever it comes from, as a positive contributor to their effectiveness and ongoing professional development. Open communication channels can help foster an inclusive, supportive environment in which team members feel valued for their contributions and are able to build upon their strengths and improve upon any areas of weakness. Despite this, many do not believe that they receive feedback on their work on a regular basis. This is often because ongoing constructive feedback is not encouraged in the workplace. Research, particularly amongst younger employees shows that people value constructive input on their work, and they want it frequently. The problem is it doesn't happen as often as it should and then, not done with the requisite skill.

Open feedback cultures engender a climate of mutual trust, which in turn encourages information to be shared, thereby reinforcing the culture. Mutual trust is the ability to rely on someone and for them to be able to rely on you. This includes reliance on character, ability or motivations. Trust within a team means that you can rely on your fellow team members to do the right thing in the right way. It minimises the amount of risk you feel when dependent upon others, in other words, makes you feel comfortable and safe within the group, the most important prerequisite for a healthy culture. Trust is essential if a group of individuals is to operate effectively as a team with the active contribution of everyone, allowing skills to be fully utilised and tasks to be completed through cooperation. Without trust, even a team made up of the most talented and knowledgeable people will never be able to perform at an optimal level.

As mentioned previously, when people feel able to freely express themselves and challenge the status quo, a degree of conflict is inevitable. Conflict is friction or opposition caused by real or perceived differences in approach or opinion and should be seen as a part of work-life. When managed effectively, conflict is positive and essential to the functioning of an inclusive team, but unfortunately it is often handled badly or avoided altogether. A degree of conflict in teams is actually a positively healthy sign. The more we develop a culture of open feedback, collaboration and shared responsibility, the more conflict is likely to arise- precisely because people care and feel able to express their opinion. A lack of conflict is often an indicator of significant problems such as overly autocratic leadership or an environment where people feel disengaged or excluded. Conflict always results in negative consequences when disagreements are glossed over, allowing them to develop into hostilities, damaging communication and souring relationships. Open feedback supported by managed conflict benefits teams as it encourages the expression of new ideas which can lead to new and better ways of doing things. It can also help to highlight issues that have the potential to turn into deep rooted problems if left to fester.

8

TRUST EVERYONE, AND TRUST NO ONE
How to create healthy risk culture

When I talk about managing risk, I am considering it beyond the bounds of what is usually considered the remit of risk and compliance functions in banks, engineering or aviation contexts for example. What I am talking about is doing what you can do to minimise the likelihood of anybody doing stupid, unethical or damaging things, and create an environment which encourages rapid and effective remedial action to be taken when they do. This is not a simple endeavour, as we saw in the example of Just Cultures, and is not as straightforward as it might at first seem. For example, when we respond by imposing rigorous risk management processes while failing to differentiate between types of mistakes this will often mean that human error or honest misunderstandings become heinous crimes. This makes them indistinguishable from the truly heinous crimes. It encourages people to hide their errors making them impossible to learn from and share. It also stops people from applying their judgement on the virtue or otherwise of their own deeds and those of the people around them. Consequently, I use the term minimise intentionally. This is because it is vital to bear in mind that people will always find a way to do the wrong thing and expecting us to ever reach a point when all risk is mitigated is totally unrealistic.

TRUST EVERYONE, AND TRUST NO ONE

While it makes perfect sense for honest mistakes to be distinguished from intentional transgressive acts, there are plenty of dangers associated with treating the latter with anything approaching zero tolerance. A compelling example of this is the universal human capacity for doing the wrong thing as painstakingly exposed in Dan Ariely's book The (Honest) Truth About Dishonesty. Ariely conducted a series of social experiments which provided evidence which challenged the prevailing view of the conditions under which people will and won't behave dishonestly. Hitherto it was assumed that people naturally sought to act in ways which advantaged themselves to the greatest extent. This was seen as entailing simple rational consideration of the relative costs and benefits of different courses of action which involved weighing up the benefits of behaving dishonestly against the chances and likely consequences of getting caught. This view provided us with two obvious ways to reduce the likelihood of dishonest behaviour namely to increase the probability of being caught and to increase the magnitude of the resulting punishment. This rationale has typically been followed by financial institutions who have sought to manage risk through increased oversight from risk and compliance functions while imposing more draconian consequences for wrongdoing. Ariely provided a compelling case that countered this view, concluding that everyone cheats, and the vast majority do so while at the same time retaining a belief in themselves as honest and trustworthy. They simply transgress to a personally acceptable degree. This is a limit we impose on ourselves and is the point below which our self-image is not compromised, something Ariely argues that this is quantifiable and consistent across all cultures. What's more, once you've justified doing something wrong, you're more likely to justify it again and even rationalise away even more extreme misdemeanours in future.

Ariely's experiments expose the dynamic tension that we all find ourselves in, which is the need to believe in our own capacity to act as a trusted member of a cohesive group, set against a motivation to behave in a way which serves our own self-interest. If true, the implications of his work for the development of an effective risk culture are clear. Simply articulating acceptable and unacceptable modes of behaviour will never be enough to prevent wrongdoing. Everyone has the capacity to do the wrong thing under the right (or wrong) circumstances, and the drivers of this are often unconscious and irrational. What we need to do is to understand what the environmental controls are that encourage people to do the right thing and implement them. The second implication is for how we respond when people do wrong. Our response would need to be much more measured and reflective of basic human nature than it currently often is if we are to avoid stigmatisation creating a further barrier to people speaking up and admitting to their own transgressions or those of others.

The conditions under which people appear to be less likely to cheat include the psychological proximity to the consequences of the deed. This depends on how close the perpetrator is to the victim. It is much easier to rationalise cheating someone you don't have a close relationship with than someone you do. The key word here once again is empathy. The closer you feel to a potential victim, the more able you are to put yourself in their shoes and see the likely harm that you will cause them personally. This makes committing the crime much more difficult for you to justify morally. Given that the ultimate victims of corporate wrongdoing are most often customers, developing a customer-centric culture is likely not only to provide a unifying sense of purpose but could also do much to prevent wrongdoing in the first place.

Ariely's book contains an anecdote about a woman who notices that her maid has been stealing small amounts of meat from her freezer on a regular basis. In order to dissuade her from further misdemeanours the woman confides in her maid that she suspects someone has been stealing from her and that as she trusts the maid above all of her employees. She gives her a small pay rise and a responsibility to keep a key to the freezer and help her to keep an eye out for the perpetrator. The thefts stop immediately. This story highlights something that has been known for a long time. If you publicly demonstrate trust in someone, the more likely they are to repay that trust. By singling out the maid as someone who had her trust, the woman increased the moral burden on her, making it far more difficult for her to justify her former behaviour. Trusting people to do the right thing while recognising their capacity to do the wrong thing may seem like a tough balancing act. But given the irrational nature of much of human behaviour, it is little surprise that many of the means we need to adopt to influence it may feel counterintuitive. We must be led by the behavioural science and recognise that the usual kneejerk response of increased external oversight coupled with the imposition of draconian punishment will actually make the situation worse.

Often, when organisations focus on the achievement of results rather than on how those results have been achieved, they end up rewarding wrongdoing. This creates a conflict of interest which allows people to justify their poor behaviour. This is commonly cited as the cause of the LIBOR scandal. The London Interbank Offered Rate is the interest rate that UK banks charge other financial institutions for short-term loans. LIBOR acts as a benchmark for interest rates for the prices of mortgages, currency and interest rate swaps, and consequently has been described as the world's most important number. The LIBOR Scandal was caused when bankers from a number of institutions were discovered to have colluded with each other and manipulated interest rates in their favour when they lent and borrowed money. Before this discovery, the poor practice was so widespread and so profitable that you were regarded as a fool if you did things by the book. If you are making loads of money and this is your main benchmark for success, then by definition, all is well in the world. From the perspective of leadership, if you're hitting your targets, why change things? And if questionable practice is not brought to your direct attention, why go looking for problems and make life difficult for yourself? This is all exacerbated by the fact that the ultimate losers were so abstracted from the perpetrators that interest rate manipulation was effectively seen as a victimless crime. When you are getting rewarded for results and nobody really scrutinises how you are achieving them, you can quickly convince yourself that what you're doing is OK and actually start to feel pretty pleased with yourself. Situations like this seem to point to the existence of something akin to Paradox of Integrity where a misplaced belief in the integrity of your actions makes you less likely to scrutinise them, thereby increasing the chances of you acting in a way that is lacking in integrity. From inside teams, normalisation of deviance can render even the most 'obvious' of indiscretions much less than obvious. Team members working in close proximity often share a collective blindness to the risks they are taking. In the absence of scrutiny from inside the group means that an external perspective is required to bring these to the surface, by which time the damage has been done. It is only then that the scales fall from collective eyes, and everyone asks the perennial question *how could we have let this happen right under our noses?*

When people operate under stressful conditions or time pressure, or when the consequences of failure are severe, a sense of urgency can cause them to make instinctive, ill-considered decisions or to take a shortcut that causes them to deviate from established best practice. If we are successful or no negative immediate consequences result, we can begin to convince ourselves that rather than getting away with taking a risk, we have actually made the process more efficient without any downside. Taking shortcuts to achieve objectives can come to be viewed as the best course of action when there is sufficient urgency. In this way over time, even behaviours that would previously be considered well beyond the established bounds of safety or probity can become the norm. The timescales for this process may be relatively short or take many years.

When you have a function that 'owns' an issue like culture and risk you're in for problems. Risk and compliance functions often focus on creating 'compliance cultures' through the imposition of strict rules and procedures. In the absence of in-group processes for reflection on their own practice, there are two likely outcomes. Where there are strictly imposed rules externally in workplaces where immediate jeopardy and stress levels are low, compliance cultures can quickly become compliant cultures. In a healthy risk culture, the highest authority are principles and values. In a compliant culture, people at the top of the chain of command are the highest authority. In compliant cultures, people stop thinking about what they're doing. They are not required to use their judgement and consequently experience a reduction in their ability to do so. In work contexts where there is stress and pressure to achieve results, an external function that imposes rules can easily come to be seen as unreasonably restricting your ability to achieve those results. Those imposing the rules can then come to be viewed as the enemy whose rules are to be circumvented and whose efforts to oversee obstructed. If you don't require people to think, use their discretion and take decisions based on their moral and ethical compasses, they will stop doing so. To say that responsibility for implementing a healthy risk-management culture lies with senior management or particular corporate function is extremely dangerous. Dilution of responsibility allied with the normalisation of deviance creates a very powerful mix. It appears however that this fact may be least apparent to those who need to understand it most. In one survey of employees within the UK financial sector, Conflux found that those least likely to believe that people should be allowed to exercise discretion in their work were those from Risk and Compliance Functions.

The typical taxonomy of a corporate failure in risk management usually consists of four distinct phases. The first is a failure in adherence to core values. This may be because the values are not adequately or clearly expressed in terms of behaviours, or more likely because people make poor decisions because they are discouraged from using their discretion while being put under stress by competing priorities or peer pressure. These are likely to include the achievement of personal or group targets, inappropriate incentives, corner cutting to achieve a particular outcome or the desire to hide errors or losses for example. Very often, it is a desire to protect the reputation of the organisation, at best a short-term strategy that will almost certainly backfire in the long run.

This is usually followed by a second phase characterised by a failure of oversight. This may be due to ineffective checks and balances, a failure to take heed of warnings and complacency caused by an overemphasis of the positive, the paradox of integrity or a *'don't ask don't tell'* mindset. While we're on the subject, one of the most brainless corporate leadership maxims of recent times has to be; *Don't come to me with problems come to me with solutions*. If you apply this principle, very soon people won't come to you with anything at all and you won't have the slightest clue about what is actually going on in your own company.

The third element is facilitated by a lack of psychological safety. This may either be an existing feature of the current culture or may emerge as a key part of the dynamic of the specific cultural failure. This is characterised by people feeling unsafe speaking up and questioning what is happening or suffering negative consequences when they do. The fourth and final stage is normalisation of deviance. This final stage can happen with remarkable ease and speed as by its very definition a repeated action which has no negative consequences for the doer will increasingly come to be seen as normal. By this stage the Rubicon could be seen to have been well and truly crossed and a sense of helplessness may set in. While the path back to a less deviant 'normal' will undoubtedly be hard, there is nothing to be gained and much to be lost by continuing to leave the situation unaddressed.

In order to disrupt this pathway we need to have the following safety nets in place.

- **Values**- clearly articulated indissoluble rules that guide our actions and decisions, and if these fail, early action can be taken if you maintain…

- **Vigilance**- a recognition that things can and will go wrong, along with a swift and proportionate response when they do. This response is only made possible within a culture of…
- **Psychological safety** and **inclusion**- a work environment where everyone feels able to admit to their mistakes, challenge, question, raise objections and propose solutions. This can be stifled by a fear of negative consequences or concerns about opening a lot of cans of worms. This tendency will itself be mitigated by a…
- **Learning focus**- a recognition that first and foremost, errors present hugely valuable learning opportunities and that seeking to bury them will inevitably come back to bite you. If you stumble at any of these steps what is ultimately needed is…
- **An understanding that it's never too late** to remedy any situation, no matter how dire, but you will need to be open and honest and you may need to seek external help. This is the only long-term way of preventing the maximum damage to your corporate reputation.

In essence, that's it. When allied to robust procedures, training and collective oversight, everything we need to help maintain a healthy risk culture is encapsulated within these five simple principles.

9

WHEN FOREHEAD MEETS WALL
Creating a coalition for change

In the early noughties I was involved with a large multinational on a brand-new values programme. The programme had board-level sponsorship and was led by the Internal Communications function aided by a fleet of external consultants. Through and exhaustive and protracted process the values were defined, honed, redesigned, rehoned, sent out for consultation, polished, branded and presented to staff through a panoply of communications channels and media. The result was three core values statements each supported by a number of behavioural descriptors, providing exemplars of precise ways that these values were to be lived. The process followed a well-established change management model which emphasised the need to build a *burning platform*, establish a *constituency for change* and celebrate *quick wins*. At one meeting deep into the process, the Head of Internal Communications announced to the assembled project team that the recent staff survey had shown that 85% of employees understood the aims of the programme with a similar percentage committed to helping it to succeed. According to him this was indeed a quick win in that it was evidence of the resounding success of the communications initiative and that the work was all but complete. The mood in the room was positively self-congratulatory.

After some discussion a decision was taken to validate this finding through a slightly different means. After all, the staff survey had been conducted a couple of months before and the results were unlikely to reflect some of the more recent communications efforts. The real situation could be even rosier that the survey suggested. A sample of employees from across the company were to be contacted by phone and asked to state the three values statements and provide a brief description of what these meant in practice. Only 15% could do so for all three. Far from being crestfallen, the Head of Internal Communications was convinced that this was evidence that the vast majority of employees had internalised the messages and the more reliable results were the initial ones. While people may not be able to parrot the precise phrasing of the values statements, they were aware of the sentiments expressed by them and the project was ready to be passed to the HR Function. HR's job was to integrate reinforcement mechanisms into the talent and performance management processes to help make sure the changes stuck. Very little resource was provided for this element of the programme, but most of the hard work had already been done, hadn't it? But the truth actually lay somewhere between these two measures of alignment, when we tested understanding using behaviourally anchored questions of the kind described in the following chapters, we found that 30% of people were pulling in the right direction, with 40% feeling no need to do anything different at all.

Recently there has been a profusion of consultancies specialising in communications and change. Just like engagement and culture, these two words appear like conjoined twins often enough to suggest that they increasingly are becoming conflated. This is evidenced by the fact that responsibility for and ownership of change programmes increasingly lies with internal communications functions. There is often a presumption that the challenge of change in general and culture change specifically, is primarily a communications challenge. If you inform, educate, and consult about the need for and nature of the change, it is often assumed that the work is all but done. This belief is given false validity through staff consultation. Organisations often rely on employee feedback as to the extent that firstly, they understand the changes required and secondly, that they feel personally motivated to adopt the changes. Anyone who has conducted employee research will know that the best way to get high positive feedback is to start a question with the words *do you know*, or *do you understand*. People simply do not like to admit that they do not understand something. This is never truer than when you ask people to indicate the extent to which they agree with statements such as *I understand what the change programme means for me in my day-to-day work*. We often find questions such as this eliciting positive responses of over 80% or 90%. This of course gives very little indication as to the true level of understanding, and if we do test this using more objective measures, we often find a very different picture. If people do not know what is required of them, commitment to do what they can to help is something you probably don't want. Better they do nothing than run off in completely the wrong direction. The reassuring thing is that more often than not, absolutely nothing is precisely what they do.

Research into the perceptions of employees consistently shows that the positivity of any opinion largely depends on the proximity of the point of reference to the individual. This effectively means that when people are responding to questions about themselves or their team members or even their local management, they are much more positive than when they're talking about other teams, the managers of those teams, and particularly senior leadership. This phenomenon is very measurable and almost universal. This has huge implications assessing the readiness for change. As we know, if you have a very positive view of the current status quo, you are far less likely to see the need to do anything differently. So, what happens when people are asked to change during a transformation programme, they will tend to believe it's an issue for somebody else and not themselves. Again, this is a very measurable, quantifiable phenomenon. For the hapless change manager who has spent huge amounts of time and resource designing communications and education materials and finely constructing that *burning platform* what they often experience is people turning around and effectively asking them '*well why don't you call the fire brigade then?*'

Habitual behaviour is very resistant to change in the absence of an alteration to the environmental precursors of the behaviour. This is why communication and persuasion alone are never enough. Culture is the assumptions that people make and behavioural norms they drive within an organisation. People quickly, and often unconsciously learn what these are and internalise them to operate successfully. The most basic thing that many practitioners and leaders fail to grasp is that words alone will never change culture. Executives who merely lay out a new corporate initiative and exhort the benefits of change will achieve very little. Beautifully designed intranet sites detailing corporate values and expected behaviours will be read by the few in the short term, but ultimately ignored by everyone in the medium to long term.

Sure, people can be resistant to change, but often the assumptions as to why this is the case are inaccurate. People very rarely dig their heels in and refuse to budge, their response is usually entirely passive as they simply don't personally feel any need to change. If we ever get to the point when we start pulling those truly effective levers of change by creating the conditions under which people will choose to behave differently, we start to hear people say some tell-tale things. That is if we actually ever reach this point and lot of change programmes never actually do. The first thing we tend to hear employees say is not '*I'm not doing that*', instead you will hear something like '*Oh, so you really want me to do this thing differently then?*'. This is the moment when an exasperated change manager who has spent an inordinate amount of time and effort in an attempt to win hearts and minds is likely to put their head in their hands or start pulling their hair out. But even then, if you think that the penny's finally dropped, you've cracked it and you've broken through, you will still have a lot more to do.

A commonly articulated 'truth' is that in order to create change you should elicit the support of influencers. These may not be leaders in the hierarchical sense, but individuals who exert a strong influence over their fellow team members. This seems on the face of it to be a sensible course of action, but we need to sound a note of caution. Influencers may actually be very effective at reinforcing the status quo, and if passive resistance to change is a characteristic of a group it is entirely likely that this is precisely what they are doing. Influencers are often the 'usual suspects' who are confident and assertive and contribute most during meetings. Your best advocates may be those less vocal team members who, on being given more of a voice may actually signal a real intent for change. It's very tempting to see newer recruits into your organisation as neophytes and induction processes as an opportunity purely to bring them into the fold. It is worth remembering though that they are, as far as insight into your culture is concerned, the frogs and that paradoxically it is the older hands that may in fact in many respects be the tadpoles. This is because new recruits bring with them a fresh perspective and may be much more capable of seeing the prevailing culture objectively for what it is. If encouraged to do so they will be able to reflect on the impact of culture upon them personally during their experience of the acculturation process. This is as true for new entrants into the world of work as for the experienced hires. During induction we traditionally focus purely on inculcating newcomers into organisational values and established ways of working. They are however the ones through which your culture can be best illuminated and explored. They are actually in many ways ideally placed to be the teachers and are a potentially valuable resource to be tapped into.

10

I SEEM TO HAVE LEFT MY LEG ON THE TRAIN!
How not to measure culture

After having spent 20 years conducting employee research, it was becoming increasingly clear to me that traditional employee surveys were not providing much in the way of benefits to many organisations, particularly when it came to measuring and changing culture. But there seemed to be very little alternative. Motivated by models that assumed that enhanced employee experience led to improved organisational performance, almost every employer of any size had jumped on the treadmill, churning out surveys year after year in the belief that somehow this would drive the organisational change that would improve employee experience, culture and by extension, business results. Employee engagement has consequently become a common term in people management, but it can mean different things to different people. The proliferation in roles entitled Head of Communications and Engagement shows how engagement is increasingly becoming associated with internal communications. Given that the primary activity of a corporate Internal Communications function is to send out messages to employees and that we never talk about '*engaging someone in a monologue*', this is not the sense in which I use the term. Instead, what I'm referring to is what we routinely attempt to measure and manage through employee engagement surveys, the thing that is supposed to confer all kinds of competitive advantages on organisations who succeed in having an 'engaged' workforce. The thing that is all too commonly conflated with culture.

The employee engagement survey has become one of the most ubiquitous people management fads of the last 30 years. It has grown into a multi-million-pound business with just about every organisation of any size conducting a regular employee engagement survey and huge numbers of conferences, articles and books on the subject. In seeking to measure culture, many organisations have deployed identical methodologies for assessing engagement, often simply in an unthinking cut and paste manner. At first sight it may appear that this is problematic purely because culture is very different from engagement and therefore it needs to be measured and managed in a very different way. In which case, developing two separate methodologies for measuring and managing both would be the ideal solution. While this is undoubtedly true, we should question whether we should be deploying engagement surveys in their current form at all. The existing methodology for measuring and managing engagement has always been so deeply flawed that we should do it properly or stop doing it altogether. Almost certainly, what we should be measuring and managing instead is culture. The trick is to do it in a way which identifies the sweet spot where there are mutual benefits for both an organisation and its employees and developing an effective methodology for change. Before we all go into much detail about a solution to this problem, it would be useful to talk about how the concepts of culture and engagement differ, and how they are related.

Much like culture, employee engagement has always been an ill-defined concept with almost as many definitions as there are people who have attempted to define it. Originally employee engagement morphed out of employee satisfaction surveys when the management consultancies decided to get involved. They quickly realised they had an opportunity to make some easy money. In order to bring these surveys into their logical remit, the trick was to link employee experience with organisational effectiveness, in other words to sell the message that if you drive up employee engagement and you'll be more profitable and successful as a business. This was supposed to provide a business imperative for spending large amounts of money on their services in terms of return on investment, rather than just simply to strive for the commercially more dubious goal of having happy employees. Other than cost savings commensurate with reduced employee turnover, just exactly how engagement resulted in business benefits was never adequately explained, and all attempts to show a clear causal link between engagement and business performance have failed.

Most definitions of engagement and measures of it do however contain common elements. These are usually that engagement is defined as a state of mind characterised by loyalty, advocacy and willingness to exert discretionary effort. Consequently, measures of it usually consist of an aggregate score from questions assessing attention to stay, willingness to recommend the employer as a great place to work and to go the extra mile to help it succeed. What makes this a particularly unsatisfying way of defining and measuring engagement is that no attempt has been made to identify what the state of mind that drives these behavioural outcomes is. This way of thinking about engagement has arisen from the measures driving the concept, of putting the cart before the horse. If we think of this in memetic terms, this is the equivalent of attempting to measure and influence behavioural outcomes without bothering to identify what the underlying basic assumptions are that are driving them.

While they are certainly related, the manner in which culture, engagement and performance interact is more complex than is often characterised. We need to challenge the simplistic assumption that culture engenders engagement which in turn drives performance. It may, but equally it may not. Can we have engagement without a high-performance culture? Yes, there are plenty of examples of work environments where employee engagement, by commonly used measures is high, but performance is not. Can you have high performance without engagement or a high-performance culture? Yes, but not for very long. Any slave driver can increase performance temporarily, but this will ultimately be unsustainable and result in damaging burnout in the long run. If you work within a successful organisation where targets are being hit, customers are happy, bonuses are being paid and the view of the future is upbeat, it's much easier to be engaged than if the organisation is struggling and the pressure is on. This is an example of business success driving engagement rather than the other way around. If this kind of success leads to a strain on resources however, the situation may be very different, with excessive demands to service a growing number of customers having the capacity to drive down engagement due to increased levels of stress or burnout. All of this shows how the relationship between culture, engagement and performance is far from predictably linear and unidirectional. Engagement is however an outcome of a healthy culture just as much as efficiency, financial performance and customer satisfaction is, but while culture is the key factor that supports both engagement and high performance, it is distinct and needs to be measured differently.

While already measuring employee engagement at regular intervals, many organisations will look for a means of assessing culture or of tracking the impact of a specific culture change programme they might be embarking upon. The temptation for many organisations will inevitably be to look to use assessment tools which are already familiar to them. The option to use existing vehicles for assessing culture can be very attractive in that they appear to provide a cost-effective and simple solution in a format that is already familiar to everyone. This usually means using their employee engagement survey as a way of attempting to understand their organisational culture. In many cases, this entails little more than a superficial name change which introduces the word 'culture' into the employee engagement programme branding. In others it may mean the addition of a few additional questions designed to address culture into a survey. This is often encouraged by engagement survey vendors who are increasingly prone to misleadingly label them as culture surveys. The problem with this approach is that culture cannot be measured through typical types of questions used in employee engagement surveys. The reason for this is simple. When we assess culture, what we need to do is to tap into behaviours and the unconscious assumptions that drive them, whereas traditional employee engagement survey questions only access those visible parts of the iceberg, the espoused values. As Schein described, these espoused values are inherently unreliable hence measures of them cannot have any real degree of validity. We have an increasing body of evidence which shows this to be the case. Despite many years of desperately trying to establish a causal link between engagement levels and organisational performance, in other words show that their measures of engagement have predictive validity in terms of business outcomes, management consultancies have consistently failed, and have now all but given up trying. In response many have moved the goalposts, dropped the term 'engagement' and are now talking about 'employee experience', an even less well-defined concept, and still without any predictive power with regard to business outcomes.

Employee engagement surveys also have a spectacularly rotten track record of predicting or even accurately reflecting other important real-world outcomes. A very obvious example comes from Mid-Staffs NHS Trust itself. For the last 20 years the NHS has mandated a staff survey across all its constituent Trusts and Agencies, of which Mid Staffs was just one. The survey is made available to every NHS employee year on year and the results from it are published annually online in full and are accessible to the general public. The results for individual trusts are league tabled and compared to overall benchmark comparators to add context. The NHS Staff Survey has a broad coverage including detailed sections on standards of care, near misses and incident reporting. Despite this, no significant differences between the responses of Mid-Staffs employees and those of other

Trusts was apparent in these areas in any of the years in the run up to the commissioning of the Francis Report. This means that even when faced with results of the shocking litany of failures detailed in the report in their everyday work, the staff survey failed to provide the employees of Mid Staffs NHS Trust with an effective means of voicing their concerns. This was the case despite employees being provided with a risk-free means of doing so. The responses to the survey are collated and analysed and reported by an external body, meaning that respondent anonymity is guaranteed. Whilst there may be concern amongst some employees that their responses could still be traced back to them, however unfounded, this alone is unlikely be responsible for the lack of sensitivity and validity of the survey as a measure of employee experience. This is not a criticism that can only be levelled at the NHS Staff Survey, it also applies to most of the employee surveys run by employers of all sizes and sectors.

When the concept of employee surveys was first developed around 30 years ago and they started to be used widely as a people management tool, care was rightly taken to ensure that they were easy to complete, report on and analyse. This was driven by a wholly laudable and understandable motive, which was the real need for everyone to come on board with working with the resulting data to drive improvement. This initial desire for simplicity resulted in standardised question formats, scales and reporting which allow for external benchmarking. The problem is that over the years we have been unable to evolve the content of surveys in any meaningful way. We are wedded to the ubiquitous 5-point Likert scale and the desire for comparisons with normative data means that we have seen in virtually no change in the wording of questions in 30 years. This has resulted in the all too familiar use of slabs of questions which never change from year to year, even when their lack of utility in informing change has become increasingly apparent.

I SEEM TO HAVE LEFT MY LEG ON THE TRAIN

Simple doesn't have to mean boring and the way we continue to design surveys is actually quite insulting to the respondents. How many times have I heard surveys being described as *'light touch'* or *'user friendly'* when these phrases are in fact euphemisms for *'we don't trust our people to be able to respond to questions that require any real effort or thought'*? The truth is that people generally find being challenged engaging and respond well when they are. Instead, we continue to present them with stultifyingly boring, repetitive lists of bland questions and response options and if they're lucky, the odd open comment question. The problem is in our attempts to develop culture assessments which are accessible to all, in many cases this has effectively meant simply cutting and pasting these methodologies and formats without ever questioning their utility or validity.

Staff surveys are almost always anonymous, with great emphasis placed on the fact that results are always reported in such a way so that nobody can be identified from their individual pattern of responses. This again was a measure implemented early in the history of surveying that has very largely remained unchanged to this day. This means that even if they wanted to, respondents cannot give feedback which can be attributed to them personally, making it more difficult to provide them with personalised feedback about their own engagement. The original reason for stressing anonymity was to encourage open and honest responses and to help achieve healthy response rates, predicated on the belief that the levels of trust between staff and leadership were not all they should be. The continued maintenance of the enforced anonymity on respondents could easily be seen to send out a message, namely *'we still believe you don't really trust us enough to give us personally attributable feedback'* and certainly does not indicate that we have made any strides forward in building open, trusting cultures. This also serves to reinforce some rather undesirable behaviour memes. Advances in how we collect and process data now means that we can easily give respondents the option of remaining anonymous or not, but very few organisations take advantage of this functionality. As we will see, providing this option gives us with a very powerful means of objectively assessing how open and trusting a culture actually is.

It is not only the format of these surveys that presents a problem, but also the way the results are presented and used. An entire industry has proliferated around standardised surveys which allow employers to benchmark their scores against those of other similar organisations. The aim of this is to prove their status in comparative terms as an *'employer of choice'* or *'great place to work'*. In practice this means doing what you can to improve employee engagement scores. In some cases, this means striving to improve the employee experience, in many others the focus is on simply improving the scores themselves. As we know, what gets measured gets managed, the uncomfortable truth is that it is often the measures themselves that are managed upwards without the requirement for any improvement in the employee experience they purport to assess. An expectation that scores will inexorably improve from year to year exerts considerable pressure on everyone, and this has even led many organisations to incentivise managers to achieve high scores from the employees who report to them. Survey scores are often incorporated into balanced scorecard assessments against which annual bonuses are determined. Under these circumstances, it is hardly surprising if managers are tempted to influence scores through fair means or foul. This is never more so than when external factors which lie beyond the direct control of people managers, such as changes to the external business environment, exert a negative impact on levels of engagement. What we really need to do is to free ourselves from the tyranny of indices, numerical targets and external benchmarks which leads to chasing the numbers rather than making the substantive changes that are required. A far more meaningful measure upon which bonuses or other incentives for managers should be based is therefore the extent to which they have taken steps to work with their people to make improvements to employee experience.

In other words, incentivise the right kinds of behaviours, not ever higher scores. Unfortunately, this is not something that happens on a regular basis.

Another obvious problem with using engagement surveys to assess culture is the underlying assumption that people telling us that everything is OK is desirable and healthy. This is not helped by the fact that questions have traditionally been constructed in such a way that an *agree* or *strongly agree* response is invariably a favourable one. This was originally done because it made reporting and interpretation easier, but what it also does is mean that the desirable response, in other words one that reflects well on the employer, is clear and obvious to everyone. This plays into all kinds of biases like social desirability, meaning that questions often receive unrealistically positive responses. These are readily accepted at face value as they are very reassuring to leadership and allow them to trumpet their credentials as an employer of choice. But what organisation would not benefit from a little constructive feedback that is less than positive from time to time? Whilst it seems to be a general phenomenon, it has always been curious to me how our response to employee feedback tends to be so different to that to customer feedback. Imagine for a moment that we were conducting a customer experience programme and at the same time as our customers were increasingly telling us that everything was great, we saw no change in customer retention, individual spend of those that chose to remain with us also remained static and we were completely failing to move into new markets. It's difficult to believe that under these circumstances we would continue to believe that everything was so fantastic after all. We would almost certainly start to question the measures that we were employing to gauge customer experience and look to change them. Customer feedback that is less than positive is often, quite rightly, seen as gold dust, as it is the best evidence we can ever have of what we need to change and how to improve. This is manifestly not true for employee feedback and why this should be the case is clear. We routinely apply incentives to encourage positive feedback from employees and at the same time congratulate ourselves when we inevitably elicit positive responses. We consistently fail to question that feedback when it is at complete odds with objective evidence. The continuing loss of key talent, persistent inequities and pay gaps are just some of the outcomes that are routinely overlooked in favour of falsely reassuring employee engagement scores. The reason for the difference lies in how we treat the two sources of feedback. Customer experience programmes are usually run by dedicated teams who track and advise customer facing staff across the business who in turn, have the responsibility to use this information to improve the experiences of the customers they serve. With employee engagement however, HR have assumed, or been given the responsibility for both measuring and improving engagement. This is despite best practice dictating that this responsibility should ideally lie with leaders and managers right across the company. In this way HR are effectively responsible for marking their own homework. No wonder they are inclined to believe positive feedback in an unquestioning way. This raises a red flag for the measurement and management of culture. If we are to delegate the measurement of culture to the HR function while also charging them with the responsibility for driving positive cultural changes, as many organisations do, then we are in danger of falling right into the same trap.

This constant quest for ever-increasing scores shows another common attribute of engagement surveys that directly conflicts with the aims we have when we seek to conduct assessments of culture. This is the assumption that high scores are inherently desirable and good. But our primary motivation for measuring culture is to inform how we might need to go about changing it, so if everyone tells us how happy they are with everything, what's going to change? Change requires dissatisfaction with the status quo. It requires a vision of a better future, of the way things could be. We know this alone is not enough to drive culture change, but it is certainly a prerequisite for change to happen. If you're constantly looking for reassurance that everything is great, people will tell you that it is and you'll get told precisely what you want to hear. In this regard, in many instances employee engagement surveys are nothing more than extremely efficient complacency generators. As we have discussed, complacency is probably the biggest barrier to change of them all, and any organisation incapable of change in today's business ecosystem sooner or later will inevitably be threatened with extinction.

This also highlights the most important practical consideration that needs to be borne in mind for anyone tempted to simply use their existing employee engagement survey to measure the impact of a culture change programme. That is how existing engagement measures will be affected, and how these changes may reflect on the overall success of the process. According to almost every change management model, an important starting point for successful change is to create a coalition for action, where everyone shares an understanding of the need for change and a shared vision for a better future state. The more successful you are at doing this, as an inevitable consequence, the lower your assessment scores relating to the current status quo will fall. This means that leadership and management across a business, who have carefully nurtured their engagement scores either through fair means or foul, will start to see them heading south. This is not a great starting point for getting them behind the process of change, neither is it an intuitive way of demonstrating the success of the process to senior leadership. Using specialised questions designed to assess culture of the kinds described in the following chapter of this book will avoid this very real pitfall. While the baseline scores will start at a lower point than your engagement scores, they will be infinitely better at reflecting the progress you are making throughout the change process, allowing you to keep all stakeholders on board and allow successes to be recognised and celebrated. This is one more key element emphasised by many change-management models.

The most obvious problem is that we know the way people tend to respond to employee engagement survey questions doesn't reflect what we know is the reality and bears no relationship to the objective evidence. This is never more apparent than in the area of diversity, equity and inclusion. Questions in this area often take the form of positively worded statements such as *I believe this organisation is committed to diversity and inclusion* with *Anyone can succeed here on merit, I feel like I belong at my company* or, most baffling of all, *I can bring my whole self to work*. Benchmarking studies show that for every one of these statements, scores are extremely positive with the proportion of employees agreeing often exceeding 75%. How can this possibly be when we know that the reality regarding the diversity of many of our workplaces is so different? For example, in 2020 there were only four black CEOs leading Fortune 500 firms and that black employees represent only 8% of managers globally. These figures haven't changed at all and in the last 15 years. In 2021 the World Economic Forum is predicted that at the present rate of change it will take 267 years to close gender and ethnicity pay gaps. We also know that up to 2/3 of members of underrepresented groups do not feel that they personally benefited from their company's inclusion and diversity programmes. These kinds of survey questions steadfastly refuse to show they have any predictive validity whatsoever and yet most organisations continue to deploy them. Worse still they very effectively reinforce the complacency that removes these important issues from focus.

So how can we explain this huge gap between perception and reality? Are we looking at a collective delusion on a massive scale? Confirmation bias theory describes our tendency to be much more receptive to evidence that confirms rather than challenges your existing beliefs, particularly regarding our own virtue or abilities, or those of the company we work for. When employees tell us that everything is fine, we are very inclined to believe them. The problem is that when we're looking at culture and change, everyone telling us that everything is great is a rotten starting point for change as nothing is likely to happen. Even in the face of compelling evidence to the contrary we can and usually do choose to believe the good news.

The other psychological phenomenon at play here is cognitive dissonance, which happens when you have a direct conflict between your attitudes and beliefs and objective evidence. We all experience cognitive dissonance at some point, but if you have this in an ongoing way you have to do something to reduce that conflict. This is because it is not possible to live with that conflict in your mind over the long term. For example, if we're working somewhere where espoused values are directly at odds with the objective evidence, or our own personal values, we can resolve the conflict in a number of ways. In the case of answering questions around meritocracy, we know that respondents experiencing cognitive dissonance are prone to reframe the question in a way that allows them to respond favourably. In this way, against a backdrop of pay inequality gender and ethnicity imbalances, what leaders and their employees are responding to is not the question as asked *I believe that everyone can succeed at my company based on merit*, but the mentally reframed question; *Do you intentionally discriminate against minorities and women?*. The more socially acceptable answer of 'no' can then usually be given to this reframed question.

Employee engagement surveys consistently show that the group with the most positive views about the meritocratic nature of their companies are senior leadership. This means that those with the greatest responsibility to be scrutinising culture, behaviours and outcomes and leading in terms of change are the least likely to acknowledge the need for it. Cognitive dissonance is likely to be a huge factor for this group. Senior leaders of our biggest institutions are the first to trumpet their organisational credentials about many issues, but particularly diversity and inclusion. Their statements of commitment to providing fair and equitable workplaces are plastered all over their internet sites. While hopefully very few of them would class themselves as racist, misogynistic, or homophobic, a great many of them still demonstrably preside over cultures where progression, development opportunities and reward are far from equitably distributed. This is a difficult contradiction to resolve psychologically, but according to cognitive dissonance theory, resolved it must be.

Let's return to how we define engagement, and particularly on how we can start to identify the underlying state of mind that results in the behaviours that exhibit high levels of loyalty, pride and discretionary effort that models of engagement neatly dodge. What is the true nature of the link between engagement and business performance? What is it precisely that encourages people to expend discretionary effort do the right things in the right way? In behavioural memetic terms, what is the underlying assumption that drives the kind of behaviours that confer real benefit on a team or business?

The answers to these questions are quite a simple, and the solution is one that I stumbled on while working with a large UK retailer. One of their core values was 'give and get' which expressed a relationship between employer and employee that went beyond a traditional transactional one. This value meant that the organisation pledged to recognise individual contributions in the context of total reward, both financial and non-financial. Core assumptions around what non-financial benefits people could expect in return from expanding discretionary effort actually predicted a range of outcomes. For example, employees who agreed that the more they put into their work, the more they got out of it in a non-financial sense, were much more likely to be high performing and loyal than those who didn't. This type of question was a much better predictor of employee retention and high individual performance than responses to seemingly more direct questions like *I intend to stay here*, or *I would recommend this place is a good place to work*. I've discovered very similar results from a range of different organisations subsequently.

The relationship between the assumptions about discretionary effort and reward and how these drive behavioural outcomes is not entirely straightforward however and will need some clarification. Let's start by posing a couple of very basic questions. For example, apart from the obvious need to feed the family and pay the mortgage, why do people go to work? Or to turn the question on its head, why are people happy to invest time and effort in activities that bring them no immediate financial benefit? You regularly see groups of middle-aged men huddled at the end of railway platforms scribbling down the serial numbers on the train engines that come in and out of the stations. A more pointless waste of time I cannot personally imagine and yet there they are, come rain or shine, sleet, hail, or snow. Of course, it matters not one bit how much of a waste of time someone like me might believe it to be, what counts is that they personally get something out of it. It may be companionship, the enjoyment of being with like-minded people who share their interests, or through some sense of fulfilment at collecting a new or rarely seen serial number that attracts people to train spotting. I on the other hand, love cooking and spend a great deal of my spare time doing it. I know many other people find it a chore and do it purely out of necessity, but in most instances, I would prefer to plan a meal, source the ingredients, and prepare the food myself than actually go out for a meal where it has all been done for me. Call me weird, but there you have it. I could conceivably get paid for it through a career in catering, but I'm happy to do it for no financial reward at all.

These examples highlight why anyone does anything they don't absolutely have to, they feel they are getting something back, very often to the extent that the more they invest in doing something, the more benefit they derive from it. This payback may be tangible, companionship, or intangible, a feeling of fulfilment, but is always driven by different forms of intrinsic motivation. The annoying people you regularly hear who have enviably interesting jobs saying how lucky they are to get paid for doing something that doesn't seem like work to them are, in every case, articulating the extent to which their intrinsic motivations are being satisfied through their work.

Extrinsic motivators such as differential reward and performance-related bonuses are designed to perform this function, and to an extent when they are executed well do so, but real performance uplift is created when they work in conjunction with non-financial, intrinsic motivators. These intrinsic motivators are well-understood and have been described with a good degree of consistency and typically include relatedness; the ability to make meaningful social connections, autonomy; individual control over what you do and how you do it, competence; the ability to perform a task well and receive recognition for doing so, and purpose; usually defined by who is benefitting from your work.

When someone joins an employer, they obviously enter into a contractual relationship with them both in the legal and psychological sense. In exchange for their time and labour, an employee can reasonably expect certain things in return. These include extrinsic motivators such as remuneration and benefits at a competitive market rate, a safe and comfortable working environment, the information and tools needed to successfully complete work-related tasks, fair management processes around performance and career progression and ethical, values-driven practices that don't conflict with personal values of the employee. If any of these elements are deficient or unsatisfactory, the employee is likely to become demotivated, their performance will suffer as a result and in many cases, sooner or later they will leave. But these extrinsic motivators, while important to get right, are merely hygiene factors. The consequences of getting them wrong will result in a negative impact, but there is no uplift in performance above a base level if you get them right. The things that really have the power to boost performance are the intrinsic motivators.

The state of mind that definitions of engagement allude to but fail to define, is the basic assumption that the more I put into my work, the more, in a non-financial sense, I will get out of it. This is the assumption that drives superior individual performance and collectively by extension organisational performance. It is where the concepts of engagement and culture converge, it is the behaviour meme for engagement. This is the state of mind through which both the individual and the organisation mutually benefit. It is what we should have been measuring and managing all along.

11

TWO STORIES, ONE INCONSEQUENTIAL

Undoubtedly one of the main reasons for the discrepancies that we see between objective measures and employee feedback on measures like diversity inclusion and risk is that affectively we have spent a lot of time and effort incentivising employees to tell us that everything's okay and we are happy when they do. In many instances organisations base management bonuses either partially or fully on employee survey scores. This is a very effective way of ensuring that we get feedback that reflects well on each of the managers and their teams. It is also an extremely effective way to reinforce complacency. To give you an example of this and to illustrate some important cultural differences between different organisations, I will share examples of how two different companies responded in very different ways to a very similar issue.

A FTSE 100 hospitality company had been conducting surveys of all its staff for a number of years, and the scores in all areas covered by the survey had increased significantly in that time. So much so in fact that the suspicions of the company conducting the survey were aroused and I was asked to investigate these suspicious response patterns. These clearly showed that in many cases the survey was being completed from the same IP address extremely rapidly with multiple surveys being completed one immediately after the other. In most of these the responses were uniformly positive meaning that 'strongly agree' was being selected for every single question. This was not just in a few cases but was extremely widespread across multiple locations and functions. Clearly there was very good reason to suspect that local managers were completing the surveys themselves and there was blatant gerrymandering on a large scale. The motivation to do this was strong as a positive response from their direct reports through the survey guaranteed each of the managers an annual bonus worth a full month's salary. When I alerted the HR Director to the situation, she decided not to investigate the matter further as in her words to do so would 'damage the credibility of the whole survey process'. Given that the credibility of the process already seemed highly dubious, and the survey and the increasing scores had both for many years been hailed as major successes for HR, what she was really saying was that this had the capacity damage the credibility of her whole department.

Contrast this response with a European engineering company of a similar size. when suspicions were aroused that a particular manager had been attempting to influence his team members when responding to their annual survey the manager was immediately questioned and upon admitting that he had indeed attempted to influence the responses was summarily relieved of his management responsibility. His demotion and the reasons for it were immediately made public.

The difference in response couldn't be starker and show obvious cultural differences between the two organisations. In the case of the engineering company, the consequences of deviating from the company's core values were made abundantly clear to all at the earliest opportunity. By contrast the hospitality company had been through the first three stages of cultural failure and were well into the normalisation of deviance phase. So much so that it would be a foolish manager to risk their annual bonus by not following the example set by most of their peers. This was far from being a minor issue as the bonus accounted for a sizable chunk of the company's annual personnel costs. If widespread gerrymandering had been proven this would have placed the HR Director in an extremely difficult position. She chose what was initially the personally least risky path, at least in the short term, but certainly not the right one. In the case of the engineering firm and to my certain knowledge no such issue ever occurred again. I do not know what the situation was going forward with the hospitality company, but I suspect the problem continued at least for a while. The reason I don't know for sure is that after having provided this feedback, I was never invited back.

12

COUNTING THE DANCE STEPS
How to measure culture effectively

Why do we want to measure culture? Not out of academic curiosity or the desire to develop a universal and comprehensive description of culture. We do it because we're seeking to purposefully change certain aspects of it in an informed and targeted way. It is unusual for an organisation to start a culture measurement programme with a generalised objective of using it to diagnose where improvement might possibly be required. The need to change culture is often exposed by a specific business need or incident with negative impact, structural or strategic change. This may be a failure in risk management which brings about financial or reputational damage. It may be a legal issue related to diversity or inequality. Often, the purpose is to assess the gap between espoused values and the behavioural reality or to better align behaviours to achieve strategic objectives. In certain cases, organisations might want to benchmark themselves against what may be considered elements of a 'high performance' culture. The truth is we will never need to change all behavioural elements that define organisational culture at the same time, to attempt to do so would be pointless. Why then would we ever seek to measure all of them at once as the assessments based on comprehensive models of culture attempt to do? If we're only interested in behaviour change that addresses an immediate need or influence our ability to achieve our most pressing strategic performance objectives, then this is what we should exclusively focus upon. Only then can we zero in on a manageable number of key behaviour memes that we are looking to change.

Despite this, as we have seen, the most common diagnostic tools all take a very broad swipe at culture and attempt to cover all the organisational elements which culture may impact upon at once. As a result, they tend to be complex and difficult for most people to interpret. A prime example of this is one commonly used assessment tool which includes no fewer than 30 different behavioural dimensions. The results are presented for each of these dimensions in terms of a gap analysis between the desired and observed culture, effectively resulting in 60 individual data points. The reporting format adheres to the unwritten but seemingly universal rule for assessments of this nature in that is looks an awful lot like a multicoloured spider's web. The assessment is a well-crafted, impeccably researched and validated instrument hosted on the latest cloud-based technology. It is built using well-established psychometric principles involving academics from a number of leading institutions. It also entirely misses the point. This is because in their desire to produce a rigorously researched and psychologically robust instrument, all the academics involved in its design seem to have lost sight of the needs of the end users. The ultimate test of any assessment tool must be the extent to which it provides a practical solution to help address the issues organisations are facing in a targeted way. This means providing actionable insight that informs real change. As we have discussed, the process of culture change needs to actively involve everyone to be truly effective. If we present culture metrics in such a complex way that all but a few specially trained 'experts' individual can interpret them and bombard them with data which is irrelevant to our most immediate priorities, then this obviously cannot happen. Behaviours are of course what we are interested in because they're observable and measurable, but we need to focus on a manageable number that are truly pertinent to our immediate organisational goals. We also need to be able to present the assessment findings in a way that is accessible to everyone to facilitate informed action at all levels from the boardroom to the factory floor and increasingly of late, remote workers in virtual teams.

What everyone requires is a clear understanding of what they need to do both individually and collectively in their everyday work to support the desired cultural change. They also need to be given an objective insight into the extent to which they are or aren't living up to the required behavioural standards. It is only then that meaningful dialogue can take place about how the conditions can be created that allow these behaviours to be encouraged and rewarded. The negative assumptions that affectively act as barriers to doing what's required must be exposed and challenged.

The questions we have always asked and alas continue to ask, fail to get under the surface of culture and instead tap into those espoused values which are inherently very unreliable. In order to understand culture, we need access the implicit assumptions that really drive behaviour, bring these issues into the open where they can be consciously addressed. If we think about how we intervene at an individual level, we talk a lot about unconscious bias and about the need for people to become more aware of their biases and how they influence behaviour with the aim of consciously reframing them. If we think about an organisation, this approach can just be scaled up to an organisational level where we can expose shared assumptions and the collective behaviours they reinforce. Bringing these into the collective consciousness is a necessary starting point for change in a very similar way. Critics of unconscious bias training may be quick to point out here that it has a patchy track record of success. But what distinguishes this approach to culture change is that the increase in individual self-awareness is not an isolated objective driven by a one-off training intervention. It is a continuous endeavour, complemented with increased understanding of the role of group dynamics, organisational processes and structures and leadership capabilities, all informed by an ongoing process of measurement. The starting point has to be to establish a baseline against which we can measure change. In order to make this happen, we need to start measuring behaviours and assumptions in a robust and practical way. To illustrate how this can be done, let's look at the issue of inclusion, how does the interplay between assumptions and behaviours relate to an inclusive workplace culture in a way that is quantifiable and measurable?

When people are in an environment where they feel truly comfortable with a strong sense of belonging to the group, they behave differently from those that don't. They respond to an inclusive cultural environment in predictable and consistent ways and are much more likely to exhibit certain behaviours than those people who feel less secure. They are more likely to ask questions, express doubt, voice novel ideas or solutions and to challenge the status quo, to take considered risks, admit to their mistakes or shortcomings as well as those of others and so on. People will do these things under the assumption that the personal consequences of behaving this way will be positive, or at very least neutral, rather than negative. This means that when you start to measure the behaviours and the assumptions that drive them you start gaining a meaningful insight into culture. If you contrast this with one of the statements that we've seen earlier '*I can bring my whole self to work*' as we saw this is a really commonly used question. I've seen it cropping up in the last 20 years all over the place in terms of surveys and I still have no real idea what this statement is supposed to mean in terms of concrete behaviours nor what the responses to it are supposed to tell us. It's a meaningless question because it gives us not clue as to what the precise behaviours that constitute '*bringing your whole self to work*' actually are. When we can define what these behaviours are, then we can start designing much more accurate and valid measurements.

COUNTING THE DANCE STEPS

Developing an understanding how you personally react to situations, respond to issues and reach decisions are skills that can be developed and honed. This self-awareness allows you to develop in the areas where you need to, to have an adaptive culture that is capable of responding in an appropriate way to a range of challenges and situations. And this is the key to authenticity. Authentic leadership and cultural authenticity go hand in hand, and this extends way beyond the relationship with your employees to that of your customers and society in general.

How do you develop this cultural self-awareness? You must start by a developing a clear understanding of culture and how it works. You need to assess where we are as individuals and groups and express this in a consistent way that everyone can understand. You need to define what good looks like and create a common understanding of where we need to go and what we need to do to get there. Crucially you need to understand predominant collective assumptions and how these reinforce behaviours, both desirable and undesirable.

The most important starting point for building cultural self-awareness is to hold a mirror up to the organisation and its people. This can only be done through an assessment of the culture which is capable of identifying the core assumptions that are driving the relevant behaviours in simple and objective terms. There are a number of possible approaches to designing such instruments, but in everything we do we need to tread a careful line to create an assessment with the power to generate the necessary level of insight while at the same time being accessible and comprehensible to everyone. This means going beyond the usual anodyne attitudinal statement ratings of the employee engagement survey, while at the same time avoiding pitfalls of the complex psychometric instruments which require training and accreditation to administer and interpret. For smaller organisations the assessment process could consist of qualitative methods of enquiry, but for larger organisations this will be a very time consuming and expensive task. The reason for this is that individuals in each team need to be presented with data of direct relevance to them. We know that if for example, a programme of focus groups is conducted in a sample of employees and the results generalised across the wider employee base, the impact is greatly diluted. This is because people tend to externalise culture often preferring to see it as someone else's issue and not directly applicable to them. This tendency is avoided when we present individuals with their own responses and highlighting where these show a gap between the way things are and the way they need to be in terms that are personally difficult to dispute. For larger organisations this can only realistically be done by conducting a large scale online quantitative research. For this reason, the focus I am taking here is on medium sized and large organisations, that is those of a few hundred employees or more as these are typically ones where the most serious cultural failures tend to manifest themselves. These are also the organisations for whom the kinds of assessment discussed here provide the greatest possible potential benefits. When we take the right approach, we can use the insights gained to generate focused conversations that raise cultural self-awareness in a consistent way across even the largest of organisations. Only then do we have the capacity to kick-start the process of culture change.

While in no way an exhaustive list, the types of questions described here are suggestions for tried and tested formats which have proved to be effective in the context of a large-scale quantitative assessment. In truth, these could equally be used in either a quantitative or qualitative assessments, but as a discipline, I find it is always best to structure and word any question first in the context of a quantitative survey. This is because in this context, the meaning of the questions needs to be crystal clear as there is little opportunity to clarify any potential misunderstandings during a quantitative survey. The ultimate value of any question you use can most usefully be measured in terms of its power to uncover underlying assumptions and initiate the right follow up conversations. In other words, its effectiveness in supporting the process of building self-awareness within individuals and the wider group. To ensure consistency across a range of different teams, the discussions need to follow a basic pre-defined structure, initiated by simple prompts which do not under normal circumstances require the intervention of a specialist moderator. These are the kinds of conversations that can be conducted within your average teams across any typical organisation and facilitated by any manager. We will return to the process of facilitating these discussions later, but for now let's focus on the specific kinds of questions we could deploy.

Questions capable of uncovering the shared assumptions that drive collective behaviours fall into a number of broad categories:

1. Questions focused on behaviours driven by established processes and procedures.
2. Questions directly addressing individuals' perceptions about the extent to which desirable behaviours are seen to be practised in their work environment.
3. Assessment of the extent to which people feel able and motivated to exhibit the behaviours which directly exemplify a desired cultural state.
4. Exposure of the assumptions about consequences which are driving key behaviours, both desirable and undesirable at an individual and small group level.
5. Exposure of the shared assumptions about what is valued and rewarded at the organisational level.
6. Contextualisation- assessment of the willingness of people to exhibit identical key behaviours within different situational contexts.
7. Direct measures of the frequency of desired behaviour as contrasted with espoused values relating to that behaviour, in other words the gap between the talk and the walk.

To understand the distinction between these types of questions, it will be helpful to use real-world examples of the context within each was designed and the specific business need it addressed. As you will see, irrespective of the type of question deployed, the starting point for the process of designing them is to identify a precise and well-defined business need and clearly define the behaviours that do and don't fulfil this need. It is certainly not a generic model of culture.

The first category of questions is straightforward, but the important thing to bear in mind is that they need to address the experience of concrete behaviours, not just attitudes or perceptions. These can be as simple as direct inquiries as to whether candidates for promotion have experienced best practice behaviours in assessment and selection for example. These could include simple yes or no responses to questions such as *'The criteria against which my application was assessed were made clear to me'* or if the candidate was unsuccessful *'I was given constructive feedback as to why my application was not successful'*. While obviously established best practices, these are often not adhered to in practice due to complacency, often driven by the paradox of meritocracy.

Usually, we would look to assess culture through slightly more complicated question construction which exemplifies the second kind of assessment. For example, if we are looking to gauge the extent to which we have a learning culture, we might want to start with the behaviours which do and don't exemplify this kind of culture. If a characteristic of a learning culture is a collective growth mindset that effectively says that anyone with a capacity to learn and grow should be able to succeed, a common barrier to this is our tendency to focus on a relatively small number of individuals on whom we lavish greater opportunity for development and progression. This often creates a self-fulfilling prophesy where the criteria for success become narrow and self-defining. Through this kind of process, we can create the following kind of question requiring the respondent to indicate where they believe the organisation is on a sliding scale between two extremes:

When selecting for opportunities for development or progression there is a clear preference for;

A small number of identified high-flying star performers vs. anyone who demonstrates a capacity to develop their talents and abilities.

Similarly, if we are looking to assess the extent to which local management are demonstrating a transactional or transformational leadership style, we could construct a similarly structured question along the lines of;

Where I work, management spend their time;

Helping us do our jobs successfully through personal support and development vs. coordinating activities and monitoring performance.

The most important feature of this kind of question is that rather than having a single statement with response scale consisting of strongly agree to strongly disagree, we have a behaviourally anchored scale through which the desirable and undesirable behaviours exemplifying the target culture are defined. This kind of question is clearer in its meaning and is much more reflective of the competing priorities that people see playing out in the workplace every day than traditional questions.

The process of designing an example of the third type of question is a similar to the one described above, but a little more involved as it addresses a very specific and sometimes unique business need. The process can be illustrated through the need for a large US based retail bank to address a deep cultural problem that was having a profound impact on its business. Feedback from its customer experience tracking began to show that customer satisfaction was falling with many customers complaining of an undifferentiated and impersonal 'computer says "no" type of experience when interacting with bank staff. It became clear that in the wake of the financial crash, the overwhelming focus on rigid rules-based decision-making was taking away the ability of customer-facing staff to exercise any kind of personal discretion when dealing with their customers. This is a great exemplification of what happens when two different core values seemingly come into conflict, when the values of integrity and customer centricity appear to become incompatible. This is far from uncommon, especially in work contexts which stress the importance of compliance.

Personal integrity of course goes beyond blind adherence to fixed rules and regulations and systems should allow for some 'flex' as and when judged appropriate. Within the business context following the financial crash, in terms of behaviour memes, the assumptions about the risks associated with deviating in any way from a prescribed course were clearly outweighing those regarding the importance of providing an individualised customer service. The tendency was not confined to the area of customer service but appeared to typify a more generalised malaise where people were becoming less and less inclined to use their personal judgement in all kinds of decision-making contexts. This was likely to result in far more widespread problems including the stifling of innovation and inhibiting effective risk management. There was a clear need to start to address this imbalance in a controlled way which didn't risk a free for all where the rulebook is thrown out of the window. While the problem was a nuanced one in terms of the recent changes to the wider business context, it was far easier to conceptualise in terms of concrete behaviours. It could be expressed in terms of the tension between two courses of action namely, to stick rigidly to the rules or to exercise personal discretion when making a decision. The trick to developing a meaningful measure of culture to address each discrete element of culture is to identify and describe the desirable behaviour in clear language that everyone can understand and observe. What is also required is a simple descriptor of the prevailing current default behaviour, and the high-level shared assumption that reinforces it. In the case of the US retail bank these were;

COUNTING THE DANCE STEPS

1. Employees need to be using their discretion more in dealing with customers when the 'right' course of action is not immediately clear.
2. What they currently do is to defer to the rulebook or more senior colleagues in many cases, even when a simple appraisal of the situation would lead them to the best course of action. This has led to an impersonal and undifferentiated level of customer service, a stifling of innovation and creating an unfulfilling work environment.
3. They do this because excessive focus on compliance has led them to believe that they risk getting sanctioned for doing anything that is not explicitly prescribed by leadership or rules.

It is important to keep in mind that no measure will perfectly encapsulate every nuance of the issue at hand. For this reason, descriptors like the ones above should be high level and generalised and as such apply to a large number of people and work situations. We don't need perfect information to make better decisions, we just need to be able to generate the kinds of conversations that lead to greater self-awareness. This allows us to create a behaviourally anchored question like the one below.

When it is unclear what to do in my work the best course of action for me would be to;

Always strictly adhere to rules and procedures vs. Always use my judgement to guide me.

There are a number of elements in the design of these kinds of item which make them practical and effective but that may not be immediately obvious. Firstly, the extremes of the scale are just that, extreme, and the respondent is required to indicate on a sliding scale where the current balance lies. This helps to ensure sensitivity in that the desired responses fall all along a continuum rather than all being concentrated at either end. Secondly, the introduction provides a very generalised context in terms of consequences. Obviously more ambitious employees will be focused on the impact of their decisions on their opportunities for progression, others will only be mindful of their ability to maintain a stress-free work life. Therefore, the contextualisation needs to be a general as possible, focusing as it does both on broad and unspecified personal and professional consequences of the two courses of action.

This kind of assessment has numerous advantages over more traditional questions. Firstly, as mentioned earlier, they are much more reflective of the real-world decisions with potential consequences that people make every day. As Cameron and Quinn emphasised, *'competing values'* are at the heart of these kinds of behavioural decisions and can only be expressed in terms of the tension between different courses of action. Simple response statements such as *'I feel able to use my discretion at work'* and an agree-disagree scale fail to take any account of this kind of tension and the competing priorities creating it. The construction of these questions is made easier as they are predicated on real, specific, and clearly defined business need. Another important key feature of a behaviourally anchored question like this is that the 'desirable' response is not immediately obvious, and only becomes clear once you understand the specific behavioural change objective it reflects. This neatly avoids some of the potential pitfalls associated with social desirability bias or cognitive dissonance.

The most important feature of questions like these however is that they are clearly expressed in terms of behaviours that everyone can understand. The utility of any question can mostly be judged on the quality of the insight and discussion that results when a group is presented with its results. This discussion must involve everyone despite their lack of background in psychological assessment or models of organisational culture. It is the anchoring of the response in simple behaviours that makes this possible. These discussions within teams can be facilitated through the use of short discussion guides that pose a few simple questions. These could include:

What are the main barriers to using your discretion more in your work?

What do you see as the most worrying potential negative consequences of using your discretion more?

In what situations do you feel compliance with rules is non-negotiable?

In such situations, is there any possible scope for using your judgement in how to proceed?

The quality of discussion that these kinds of prompts encourage in conjunction with real team-specific data about the ability and motivation of people to act in support of the desired cultural change is usually far more focused and constructive than traditional 'action planning' discussions. Imagine for example that we were presenting people with the result that 76% of team members felt able to use their discretion at work, which is the actual aggregate benchmark average for this question. Under these circumstances, the issue would be unlikely to even register with the team as one worthy of discussion. Complacency would be the clear winner.

There's a second part of the question that we can ask using identical behavioural descriptors on the same scale and it is this:

If we want to maximise our performance as an organisation, what should we be doing more or less of relative to what we do now?

This question essentially asks, should we use our discretion more, should we rely more on the rules to guide us, or have we got the balance right currently? This is an important part of the question because it indicates the extent to which people feel a need for change or are aligned to your objectives in the context of a culture change programme for example. If they are they indicate a belief that we need to move to the right, it not only tells us that people probably objectively understand your change objectives, but believe it is the right thing for the business. Those bland anodyne questions like *I understand what the objectives of the change programme mean for me,* are worse than useless and do nothing to assess understanding or motivation to change. What Conflux found when employees were asked this behaviourally anchored question is that 35% of people appreciated what change was required and were effectively motivated to pull in the right direction. 20% of employees said they believed that people needed to stick even more rigidly to rules when making decisions, effectively exposing their misalignment with the change strategy. The remainder, a whopping 45% saw absolutely no need to do anything different at all. These are effectively the 'complacent' group who, if allowed to prevail, will be the biggest barrier to progress. What was of particular interest here was if you changed the reference point for second part of the question from the organisation to *my team,* this complacent response was even higher at 55%. This is a clear illustration of how many tend to see the need for change as someone else's problem rather than their own. The responses across different demographic groups were also very illuminating. Whilst senior leadership were the most highly aligned group, middle management were in fact less well aligned than non-managers. The group with some of the highest levels of misalignment were members of the Risk and Compliance function.

When you present these results back to individual teams, it clearly reinforces what people need to be doing in the context of the culture change programme. It objectively presents the percentage of people are not behind what we want them to do, either because they feel a need to move in the wrong direction or more likely are not motivated to do anything at all. This also leads to an intensely practical conversation within the group about what we need to do to get everyone behind the initiative. Again, compare this with a positive response to the more traditional question '*I understand what the aims of the change programme mean for me*', for which the benchmark figure is around 80% and the kind of discussion that this would, or rather wouldn't generate.

Results to traditional questions are not always so positive of course. When this is the case however, the discussion generated can easily be met with a defensive response, especially from management. Often, in such cases the conversation is focused on what the question actually meant and what people were thinking about when they answered it rather than what do we need to do about it. The clarity of behaviourally anchored questions help you avoid these kinds of side-tracks and allow you to move straight into some practical discussions.

By contrast, imagine if you are a manager of a team charged with presenting the findings of a cultural assessment and generating ideas for action with your team members. You are presented with a multicoloured spider's web with index scores for dimensions like Universalism, Particularism, Adhocracy or Uncertainty avoidance. It may seem like a patently ridiculous position to place a busy team leader in, but I know of many cases in many different businesses where this very thing has happened. It's not hard to see that under these conditions, not only does no positive change result, but the whole process of assessing and managing culture begins to lose all credibility. Similarly, you are presented a results report that shows that 45% of people agreed with the statement; *I am able to bring my whole self to work,* an all-too-commonly advocated question for use in assessments into diversity and inclusion. In this instance the conversation inevitably starts with completely justifiable question, which is, 'What is that supposed to mean?' often followed by a sarcastic comment from someone at the back saying something along the lines of 'I appear to have left my left leg on the train'. Hardly the best way to start a constructive and focused conversation.

The fourth way to get beyond espoused values and get to implicit assumptions is incredibly simple and remarkably effective. It's essentially to ask why people do things. This is of course the most direct way to get to people's assumptions they're making in terms of what drives their behaviour, and as such can be very illuminating. This is obviously a type of open question, and while questions of this kind are used routinely within qualitative research, they have rarely been used in quantitative assessments. This may seem difficult to believe, but the reason for this is that the answers to an open question like this have traditionally been seen as very messy, with the answers potentially covering a wide range of issues which are difficult to predict and therefore to provide pre-coded response categories for. Recently however, artificial intelligence has given us a very clever solution to this problem through text analytics, through which we can 'train' systems to automatically code responses into categories. This is an iterative process, but one that can ultimately provide a vastly quicker and more accurate means of assigning comments to categories than by using human judgement.

One simple example of this kind of question relating to inclusion is to ask the question; *Have you put yourself forward for a more senior or better paid post in the last year,' yes or no?*, and if you haven't, *why not?* Analysis of free text inputs has shown us that over 95% of responses will fall into one or more of the following broad categories:

I am happy in my current role

I was not aware of any suitable opportunities available to me

The benefits were outweighed by the additional demands and responsibilities of the role

Or

I didn't believe my application would have a chance of being successful

This last assumption can be based on a number of possible reasons including:

I felt I needed to improve my knowledge or skills before I could successfully apply

I didn't feel I had the necessary qualifications or experience

I don't believe I fit the expected profile of someone at a more senior level

When you analyse the feedback in terms of the options that people choose, you find some very powerful assumptions which are driving individual behaviours. For example, if we look in more detail at the responses falling into the category '*I don't believe I fit the expected profile of someone at a more senior level*' we find that on average marginally more females give this as a reason than men but when we look intersectionally, at women of colour, the gap typically increases to 27%. Differential responses to; *The additional responsibility and demands outweighed the potential benefits*, highlight issues around work life balance and caring responsibilities which often predominantly impact upon women to the greatest extent. Responses to; *I felt the need to develop my knowledge and skills before I could successfully apply* are again often highest for female respondents, but the benchmarked deferential between the overall average and responses from women of colour is a massive 25%. When we consider responses to; *I didn't feel I had the necessary qualifications or experience,* on average roughly 30% more women give this as a reason for self-excluding from promotional opportunities than men. While these are overall findings, some organisations show very small differentials between the responses of people from different groups, others very large ones. It is the size of these differentials which give the lie to the underlying culture with regard to inclusion. These response gaps provide a great objective and quantifiable metrics that can be used for comparative purposes and tracked over time.

So here we have a powerful example of how assumptions are driving behaviours, simply exposed through asking people *Why?* in this case their reasons for not putting themselves forward for progression opportunities. The power of this approach is that the differential behavioural response between groups readily exposes deeper cultural truths. Many HR leaders I have presented such data to have been quick to assert that these are explicable by some universal difference between men and women and as such do not reflect the culture within their organisations. This is manifestly not the case as in some organisations there is little or no such difference between the responses of men and women, while others show very large differences. It is the extent to which these organisations have an inclusive culture is defined by these differential behaviours and assumptions and can be quantified by them. In fact, our research has shown that the size of this differential is a good predictor of many structural inequalities including pay gaps and gender or minority group representation at senior levels.

The fifth type of question is rather more complex in construction, but essentially these examine the collective assumptions that people have about their organisation and its values. We have met this example already and it relates to leadership traits and inclusive leadership, and this was part of a series of studies conducted by Conflux a couple of years ago with organisations across a range of different sectors. The example referenced earlier in the book was from the NHS, but we have found this method of enquiry extremely illuminating in many different organisational contexts. Essentially, what this question seeks to do is to assess the extent to which an organisation is seen as favouring traditional traits in terms of what it rewards and values within its leadership. These traits fall into two broad groups, the first group are transactional traits which contribute to individual effectiveness, the second group are transformational traits that contribute directly to the effectiveness of others. Transactional traits include confidence, assertiveness, competitiveness and decisiveness. Transformational traits include empathy, compassion, collaboration, humility and open-mindedness. The most important traits for inclusive leadership are universally of the transformational type, but these do need to be balanced against the need to achieve results. There is a huge body of evidence which shows for example that widely held stereotypical views of what constitutes a masculine style of leadership strongly emphasises transactional traits over transformational ones. Transactional traits are important in terms of getting things done and are associated with traditional views of leadership. Transformational traits are qualitative in nature and describe how things get done. While these two groups of traits may sometimes be seen as contradictory or mutually exclusive, they are emphatically not. They do in fact complement one another, and effective leadership in a modern context depends upon having a healthy balance between the two types of traits, either within leaders or across leadership teams.

While we would certainly not want leadership teams in a healthcare setting who are full of ditheringly indecisive handwringers who are wracked with self-doubt, we would equally not want overbearing, insensitive bullies. The importance of having a balance between both sets of traits is obvious when we look at traits in isolation and in combination. For example, competitiveness without collaboration is me against the world, dog eat dog, with collaboration it is 'us' trying to be the best we can be, in other words a much more constructive form of competition. Self-confidence without humility is arrogance, decisiveness without open-mindedness is dogma, being demanding in the absence of compassion can easily turn into bullying or exploitation and so on. I'm sure you can come up with a few more of your own. Looking at traits in this way allows us to develop a very nuanced and balanced view of effective leadership in terms of getting results, but doing so in the right way, in line with our cultural aspirations for developing psychologically safe and inclusive workplaces.

In order to establish what NHS staff believed about their employers' valued in leadership, Conflux surveyed nearly 6,000 respondents by presenting them with a list of traits and asked to rank them in order how valued and rewarded they believed each was in decisions around recruitment, promotion and reward in their workplaces. What we found was assumed to be valued and rewarded most were the transactional traits of confidence, assertiveness and decisiveness. Of least value in talent management decisions were seen to be the transformational traits like humility, compassion and empathy. When we plotted those ratings against how inclusive these traits were considered to be by the respondents, we found a very linear relationship. Effectively the more inclusive a trait was seen to be, the lower the value placed on it. This relationship held true for all groups of employees regardless of seniority, role and gender. This finding is also consistent with results obtained from other similar studies across different sectors and countries. What's more, the strength of this relationship can be expressed as a single number, a correlation coefficient. This quantification allows us to compare different organisations, different groups within an organisation and track change over time. When we map this number for different organisations against consistent and objective measures of diversity and equality, for example these employers' gender pay gaps we find another very strong relationship. In other words, the extent to which employers are seen to favour transactional over transformational leadership traits is a very good predictor of the size on the pay gap. This predictive power is not something we see with traditional survey questions.

When we consider this finding in memetic terms, of assumptions driving behaviours, we can start to see the likely impact. If I'm making a decision about somebody being promoted or brought into the organisation at a senior level while harbouring this assumption, I'm very much more likely to err on the side of an emphasis on confidence, assertiveness or decisiveness for example. Any candidate for a senior position emphasising their compassionate, empathic, and nurturing side, would be much less likely to swing it in their favour. Conversely, if I am someone putting myself forward for that senior position I would be well advised not to dwell on my modest, empathic, compassionate side but to emphasise my confidence, assertiveness, and decisiveness.

The assumption about what is valued in leadership also influences the way job descriptions and advertisements are worded as well as competency frameworks and performance management criteria. All of this helps to ensure that senior teams are homogeneous and very much skewed towards more traditional leadership stereotypes. This tends to result in predominantly white male leadership teams, and will almost certainly have a negative impact on quality of the decisions that are being made.

There was a second part of the question in which respondents were presented with the same list of traits and asked to rank these according to what they believed their employer should be valuing and rewarding if organisation is to perform at the highest possible level. When we did this, in the case of the NHS we uncovered a totally different profile. People of all employee groups consistently indicated they believed that their NHS Trust should be valuing open mindedness, compassion, and empathy above everything else. Individual traits like competitiveness and assertiveness dropped right off the agenda. Essentially what people were saying was that there was a real appetite for change in terms of what we need to be valuing and rewarding in leadership. Despite the universality of this view across all of the NHS's employee groups of what should be, it was the collective assumption of what the organisation as a whole actually valued that really determined outcomes. This clearly illustrates the power of culture to influence people's decisions, often in ways which conflict with their actual beliefs and personal values. It also shows how different collective culture can be from the sum of its individual parts. It's the shared assumptions about the current reality that drive behaviour, not a shared belief about the way things could or should be. So much for our famous consensus building or the need to create a burning platform.

The NHS Charter explicitly lists Compassion as a core value, but the prevailing situation that NHS staff were describing is very much in conflict with this. What this kind of assessment effectively quantifies is the extent of the gap between espoused values and the perceived reality. The power of this approach is that it allows us to bring this mismatch to the surface and present it in very clear very meaningful terms that everyone can start to act upon. It also makes clear that there is already a consensus for change.

Conflux has now conducted this type of assessment across a range of organisations and sectors. Examining the differences in findings and what they tell us are important as they show the discriminatory power and practical utility of this approach. For example, when we conducted the same assessment within an investment bank with a very different culture from that of the NHS Trusts, we found a very different picture. While we found an even stronger perception that it was transactional leadership traits that were most valued in leadership, when we asked what we should be valuing, the profile was virtually the same. In other words, people essentially said that in emphasising traits like confidence, decisiveness and assertiveness, they were valuing the exactly the right things and that there was no need to change at all. Clearly the investment bank was in a very different place from the NHS trusts and required a very different form of intervention to start the process of culture change.

The next question type is scenario based and is designed to assess the relative willingness of people to exhibit key behaviours within different cultural contexts. Scenario based questions have obviously long been used in situations such as recruitment interviews as a means of assessing a candidate's suitability for a role. They have the advantage of providing a realistic context that is likely to be faced at work, and usually require more thought than just a simple yes or no or multiple-choice type of response. In a selection context, situational questions typically require candidates to provide an in-depth answer about how they would respond to a theoretical situation that you could face in the job they are applying for. These questions can be effective in assessing whether they possess the requisite skills or experience to deal effectively with a difficult situation for example, or could also be used to assess alignment with an organisation's values. In this last context, such questions would on the face of it seem to have the potential for application in culture assessments.

Attempting to use such questions within the context of a standardised, qualitative culture assessment can at first sight seem problematic. They usually rely upon a relatively detailed description of a situation, which can make them complicated to draft and time-consuming to complete. This problem is compounded by the fact that the lack of an interviewer means that the context needs to be very clearly described as there is no opportunity for clarification. Similarly, there is no opportunity to probe the responses given or to ask for additional detail, meaning that a list of possible responses needs to be provided which also must be precise, distinct and unequivocally desirable or undesirable for the purposes of analysis. This last requirement can effectively signal which response is the 'correct' one and thus allow the respondent to manipulate their answers accordingly.

With care, we can however design simple, contextualised situational type questions which serve to illuminate organisational culture. I find these are best done by using a two, or more part, question addressing the same issue, but changing one or more aspects of the context which allows us to analyse the difference between the responses. Below is an example of a pair of questions used in conjunction as part of a recent study to assess the extent to which people are prepared to speak truth to power in the context of inclusive culture. In other words, one measure of psychological safety.

> Part 1 -*If you were to witness unfair or discriminatory behaviour from a work colleague, the best course of action for you would be to:*
>
> *Immediately challenge the colleague yourself vs. leave it to someone more senior than you to challenge your colleague.*

COUNTING THE DANCE STEPS

Part 2- *If you were to witness unfair or discriminatory behaviour from a senior manager, the best course of action for you would be to:*

Immediately challenge the senior manager yourself vs. leave it to someone more senior than you to challenge the senior manager.

It is a good idea to have the two parts of this question in different sections of the questionnaire and whilst the absolute scores for each question will be of interest, it is the difference between the two that really exposes the assumptions which are driving the likely behaviours in each context. On average there is a twenty-percentage point difference between the responses to these questions, with senior managers being much less likely to be challenged. The bigger the gap, the less ability people feel to speak truth to power, for fear of less than positive consequences for themselves if they do. We do not need to specify the imagined consequences. These are likely to vary from person to person and can be explored later when the team discusses the survey findings. Note that the alternative to challenging the behaviour yourself is to a large extent both morally neutral, in that you are given a good reason to rationalise not speaking up within the context, and reflective of the decision-making process of people when placed in a situation where the bystander effect can kick in. We could for example simply ask if people believed they would challenge any perceived unfairness or discriminatory behaviour they were to witness. This is indeed a common type of question, but it is invariably one that universally receives a very high positive response, largely because the right, socially acceptable response is obvious, and people generally prefer to think of themselves as inclined to do the right thing. We know however that in many contexts people will not and do not speak up. It is a reluctance to do so that allows many issues to go unidentified and unaddressed, thereby allowing them to become entrenched and normalised. In this way, it is just another example of a question which can provide a false sense of security and reinforce unrealistic complacency.

The final assessment type is a direct measure of the frequency of desired behaviour contrasted with espoused values relating to that behaviour, the difference between what people say they will do compared to what they actually do. Put simply, matching the talk with the walk. This kind of measurement may seem beyond the scope of a quantitative survey, but it is possible. The most obvious and powerful example applies most directly to the assessment of a risk culture and is created in the following way.

Traditionally, surveys of employees have been conducted confidentially, meaning that processes in data collection and reporting are put in place to guarantee that nobody can be identified from their individual responses. This has been standard procedure to help ensure that response rates are high, and that people feel confident in responding openly and honestly. Increasingly however, survey responses are matched with HR information system data held on individuals. These include things like latest performance rating or recent career history, which provide greater richness and context in the analysis of their responses. To do this, we need to have data that is individually 'attributable', allowing us to know what survey responses to combine with individual records. Having matched the different data sources, we can then remove any identifiers which may threaten confidentiality before the data is processed. Conducting attributable surveys provides us with an opportunity to be much more sophisticated in terms of how we deal with the issue of confidentiality than before. What we can do is give people the option of choosing whether their responses are treated in confidence or not. In its simplest form this means asking people, usually at the end of the survey, whether or not they would prefer their responses to remain anonymous, or if they are happy for their responses to be attributed to them personally. This could for example provide an opportunity for their responses to be subsequently followed up as appropriate if they agree to it. The extent to which people are happy to have their responses attributed to them personally does of course give us a direct measure of psychological safety, and a large percentage of respondents saying they are, is a positive sign of a healthy culture. But what gives us a really deep insight into culture is comparing this with the responses to other types of questions.

Hopefully you will have gathered by now that I am extremely disapproving of the uncritical use of employee engagement survey questions in an attempt to assess culture. There are however certain circumstances under which I would advocate their use as they can be extremely useful in quantifying the gap between espoused values and actual behaviour. It is rightly of concern when people tell you they don't feel safe standing up and challenging things in their workplace, especially when they eschew the opportunity to provide attributable feedback when given the opportunity to do so. It should be of much greater concern when they assert that they are happy to, but when given the chance to, they don't. In one study recently conducted by Conflux, the percentage claiming that they would always speak up and voice their opinions at work was 82% while the percentage indicating that they would be happy to have their survey responses attributable to them stood at 22%. While this is not a perfect measure, it is a strong indicator of a considerable gap between how people say they will behave and what they are actually prepared to do. This is precisely the cultural profile which will lead to everyone telling you everything is fine when it clearly isn't and is a response profile that should raise any number of red flags. This result was extreme but still, we regularly see response differentials of 40% or more between these types of questions. Validating this kind of assessment takes time as we have to match scores against actual incident reporting, or lack thereof. We are still in the process of evaluating the predictive power of this type of analysis, but initial evidence suggests that this could be a very effective tool in early detection of areas where potential issues could lie undiscovered and addressed.

13

MIMI'S STORY CONTINUED

The weeks pass, and as part of the Innovation Programme, Mimi and her team are discussing the results from the culture assessment which she and all of her colleagues completed the week before. The results clearly show that like her, many of her team-mates are also holding back. It becomes clear that, albeit unwittingly, many are failing to support the aims of the change programme, still more are failing to recognise that they need to change their behaviour in any way. She hadn't looked at it this way before, after all the programme was being managed by HR and hadn't really affected her. The Team Manager seems a little surprised about the results too. After all, the in the annual employee survey, 80% of people had said they understood what the aims of the programme meant for them. Clearly few of them do. In the same survey, the vast majority of employees also said they believed it was safe to speak up and challenge things. Despite this, still many don't. Obviously, something needs to be done.

The ensuing discussion is different from any Mimi had been involved in since she joined the company. At the end of the meeting, they agree a way forward as a team. Together they have identified some of the main reasons team-mates feel reluctant to contribute as they could. Most importantly, she is now conscious of how she is falling short and is starting to think about how she can contribute more. Mimi and her colleagues have now not only got permission to speak up, they are positively expected to and by common agreement, nobody will criticise them when they do.

The team is also shown more ways that they can contribute their suggestions, access more information about the new programme and find out what other teams are doing. They don't have to wait before the follow up assessment scheduled in six months; they can start now. This is only the beginning. Mimi's assumptions have been shaken, as have those of her colleagues and Team Manager. Similar discussions are taking place at every level right across the organisation. It will of course take more work to change these assumptions for good, but the process of culture change has finally begun in earnest.

14

UNCOVERING CORE ASSUMPTIONS
The power of asking 'why?'

As part of a culture change programme, I was interviewing the Group Head of Customer Experience from a major airline. We got on to the topic of involving employees more in the process of change and the Executive, a board member blurted out;

'It's a complete waste of time asking employees for suggestions- we've tried it many times and most of what we got back was complete crap!'

This is a sentiment I have heard expressed many times before and was keen to get to the bottom of why he felt this way.

'Why do you say it was crap?'

'I don't know…. I suppose it's because most people have no consideration for business constraints under which we operate.'

'What makes you say that?'

'Well, if we'd have implemented most of the ideas, sure it would have been great for our customers, but we would have quickly gone bankrupt.'

'Why do you think they don't have a more realistic view of what's commercially viable?'

'Well, obviously because they don't have any real understanding of the business realities that we face'

'Why not, wouldn't one solution be to raise awareness of the kinds of constraints you're talking about?'

'We don't really want to involve ourselves in these kinds of discussions with them. They've got enough to worry about already without having to think about how the business runs, that's the job of senior leadership'

It was the final statement which exposed the key assumption that was preventing any real change from happening. It took some digging to get there, and this dialogue shows the benefit of following the 3-year-old child's inquisitorial technique that all parents will be familiar with. This simple technique of repeatedly asking *Why?* gradually peels away the layers of belief which often mask the core fundamental assumptions that drive behaviour, if it doesn't get so annoying that the questioner gets throttled. This is an example of how a memeplex can be deconstructed to allow the core assumption underpinning behaviour to be exposed and thereby potentially challenged. This deconstruction exposed how the perceived likely outcome of the process of seeking to change the prevailing culture was being used as justification for reinforcing it. This is a one very common mechanism by which the cultural status quo is maintained, and change is made much more difficult. Exposing this particular example of circular reasoning subsequently led to a much more fruitful conversation with the airline executive than would otherwise have been the case, in that it increased his level of self-awareness regarding some of the core assumptions he was making.

Asking people to tell you why they did something may seem like a perfectly simple request, but it can actually pose a question which can be very difficult to give a straight answer to. Often behavioural responses to certain situations are so conditioned that they are given no conscious consideration whatsoever. In other situations, cognitive short cuts are taken. In his famous book *Thinking fast and Slow*, Daniel Kahneman describes two distinct information processing and decision-making pathways. The first is rapid, automatic and based on heuristics, or generalised rules of thumb. The second is much slower and based on conscious reflection and consideration for the achievement of overall high-level objectives. When there is cognitive overload due to time pressure or competing priorities, the default pathway is much more likely to be the first. While this undoubtedly results in quicker decision making, a reliance on this more rapid system holds greater risk of a poor decision being made, as well as one that is at odds with our core values. It is likely to be automatic, without conscious awareness or scrutiny of the reasons for a particular course of action. The reality of the fast paced and pressurised modern workplace unfortunately means that there is always potential for poor decisions to be made. Many factors can place a strain on people's ethical and moral anchors. Stress, time or budgetary constraints, competing priorities can all contribute.

As Kahneman stressed, the comparatively risk-free decision-making pathway involves a process of conscious reflection. While this may not always be possible in real-time scenarios where quick decisions are required, there are always opportunities for more leisurely and considered contemplation later. Consciously programming regular opportunities for this type of reflection, possibly as part of scheduled team meetings is one simple way to help ensure future decisions are of a higher quality. The simple process of talking about assumptions and behaviours, why people do things is the first simple step to building self-awareness, but one that is rarely implemented in many organisational settings.

Evidence is growing that there is an even more fundamental reason why people are unaware of why they do things. The growing discipline of neuroscience is uncovering some extremely surprising evidence about why people do or don't do things, and the extent to which they are aware of what motivates their behaviour. The rapidly growing body of research into interoception is providing some fascinating insights into why people behave the way they do. Interoception is often described as the seventh sense after hearing, sight, smell, taste, touch and proprioception. It is the sense of the internal state of the body and is strongly linked to self-awareness and physical and psychological wellbeing. This sense includes the ability to read internal cues such as heartrate, muscle tension and breathing. Recent research into this sense has given us new insights into why people behave the way they do and why, in many instances they are completely unaware of the reasons behind their actions.

To illustrate how this works, imagine you are walking through a field. You see an angry bull coming for you, you take fright and start running away. A very natural and sensible reaction under the circumstances, but the pathway between stimulus and action is a little more complex than it may at first seem. What actually happens is the following. You see an angry bull, your heart rate and blood pressure increases, then as a result you feel afraid and start running away. The surprising thing is that the physiological reaction measurably precedes the emotional one. You automatically interpret the cause of the physiological response in the most appropriate way given the circumstances, and then take the relevant action. In many situations however, the appropriate emotional reaction is far less obvious than that when you encounter an angry bull. Roller coasters for example elicit very different emotional responses in different people. One person's psychological reaction to the physiological response to being flung around at high speed is one of elation and intense excitement, while another's may well be one of abject terror. In most situations, such as within our workplaces, stimuli are less extreme and our reactions to them are much more subtle. In many cases so much so that we're not even aware of what's happening. In these cases, there is a lack of awareness of the communication between brain and your body.

UNCOVERING CORE ASSUMPTIONS

Many people describe this as having a 'gut feeling' without knowing why, but these gut feelings are still powerful in building the assumptions that will inform future behaviour when the situation is encountered again. Belonging is a very good example of this, some situations just feel comfortable and supportive while others do not. We have difficulty recognising the impact culture is having on us personally, not because it is complex or intangible, but because it is subtle, and we are not attuned to the physiological reactions that define it. Studies into interoception show that while we are simply unaware of precisely why we do things in many situations, we have the capacity to become much more so, if only we take the time to become more attuned to the constant communication between body and mind.

The question *Why?* is often a surprisingly difficult one to answer. Very often, when you ask someone why they did something, you will hear a pause, followed by the same five words; '*I don't know, I suppose....*'. This construction is not just an idle turn of phrase, it is very telling. People genuinely don't know and need the time to be able to reflect on their assumptions and motivations in order to start to attempt to tell you why. This is not a question we ask people in work settings nearly enough and when we do, we often do it in a way that can easily be construed as confrontational or accusatory. The conscious act of reflecting on behaviours and assumptions is essential to the process of gaining cultural self-awareness, we must encourage people to do so much more regularly in a safe and supportive environment. This means scheduling regular opportunities for everyone to take time out of the normal routine to reflect on practices, assumptions and behaviours. This is the equivalent of taking yourself out of the immediate work context to enable a more objective and considered view of what implicit assumptions are really driving your behaviour. In other words, peeking underneath the surface at the submerged ice.

COUNTING THE DANCE STEPS

15

PUTTING THE RIGHT MUSIC ON
How do we change culture?

Anyone who has travelled on the London Underground will be familiar with the passenger announcements which are bellowed at you through the tannoy at every station stop. These are intended to help make the job of transporting millions of passengers across the city every day as efficient as possible, but their wording betrays the way they see us, not as individual commuters but as something very different.

> *'Use all the available doors'*
>
> *'Use all the space inside the carriages'*
>
> *'Use the full length of the platform'*

The problem is, I wouldn't ever want or need to use all the available doors, I only need to use one, or at least only one at a time. If I used all the space inside the carriages, where would all my fellow passengers go? Besides, how big do they think I am? And as for the full length of the platform, well you get my point.

188

When we are being spoken to in this way we are clearly not being seen as individuals. This is because London Transport utilises crowd control models which focus on 'flow', viewing individuals as part of a depersonalised mass, with properties and movement more akin to a liquid than a group of individuals. In other words, me, my fellow passengers and anyone using the London Underground are treated very much like an amorphous blob.

When we begin to look at culture through the lens of measurement and management, we are in danger of adopting a similar perspective, particularly when we are dealing with large amounts of quantitative and qualitative data collected from employees. We can very quickly forget that what we are looking at are individuals, rather than a blob. Just like the London Transport announcements there are tell-tale signs of this wherever we look in terms of how we approach the assessment of culture. We collect data from large numbers of people, report it back at high levels in aggregate rather than to individual respondents, develop metrics for internal and external benchmark comparisons and conduct advanced analytics to identify key drivers of outcomes. We then apply high-level interventions to change processes, procedures, and structures in response. All of this serves to abstract our measures of culture and how we use them from individuals to the organisational or group level. This runs counter to most of what we know about individual and group behaviour and how we influence it.

The study of group behaviour is central to the discipline of social psychology. In large part, the focus has been on how and why people are prone to behave differently within groups than they would if they were acting as individuals. This is a common theme that runs through a number of observable and well-researched psychological phenomena. While there can be some positive consequences associated with the psychology of group behaviour, more often than not membership of a group exerts an undesirable effect on the individual. For example, when individuals become part of a larger group, they can begin to lose their usual moral compass and become willing to do things or take extreme decisions that under other circumstances they would never do or would normally believe to be wrong. In other situations, they will often remain inactive or silent when they would normally intervene or speak out. These phenomena include deindividuation, the bystander effect and groupthink, for all of which we have developed an understanding of how they work and how their effects can be mitigated. In a similar way the culture of a group is very different from the sum-total of all the people who make it up, and it too exerts its effects so powerfully that people within a group culture are often influenced in a way that causes them to behave in direct conflict to their own values, often without their conscious awareness. In the case of culture however, we have been much less successful in developing effective ways of managing it and mitigating some of its more negative impacts, but there is much to learn from how we deal with other aspects of group-behaviour. Let's briefly examine what we know about each in turn.

Deindividuation is a psychological state that can occur when an individual is a member of an unruly crowd for example. They can easily become so immersed in the norms of a group, that they begin to relinquish their sense of personal identity and responsibility for their actions. Initially, it was believed that this was purely due to an increased sense of anonymity that led to a weakening of the normal behavioural constraints caused by concerns about the judgement of others. More recently there has been an increased focus on the role that reduced self-awareness has on the process of deindividuation. The greater an individual's involvement within the group is, the more self-awareness is reduced, which also distances them from their morals and their usual behavioural norms which become supplanted by those of the group as a whole.

The combination of anonymity and reduced self-awareness creates a heady mix. The reduced concern about the impression your behaviour creates in other people, along with a diffusion of personal responsibility, leads to a reduction in the normal standards of behaviour and a lowering of inhibitions. The normal focus on an individual's moral compass can become lost, letting external environmental cues govern behaviour rather than personal morals or beliefs. Role models within the group start setting behavioural norms. This way, if an individual is focused purely on the group, their level of self-awareness decreases, meaning that they are less able to monitor their own behaviour thereby increasing the likelihood of questionable or antisocial behaviour. Conversely if an individual retains self-focus, they will continue to act according to their own values, making such behaviour far less likely.

The first step in reducing the process of deindividuation is therefore to help people maintain self-awareness, even when acting as part of a group, by remaining cognisant of their own morals and values throughout. This allows people to be mindful of the lines they are unwilling to cross at all times. If we want to reduce the potentially negative effects of deindividuation, we need to help group members retain a focus on their identity as individuals and look for ways to make them more self-aware. This means helping them to examine their specific actions, the assumptions that drive them and the impact of their behaviour on others.

The bystander effect is something that occurs when an individual, who would normally intervene during an incident, is discouraged from doing so by the immediate presence of others. The incident may take the form of a medical emergency, an assault or some other form of crime in progress. Whatever its nature, the greater the number of bystanders, the less likely it is for any one of them to provide help to a person in need of assistance. This may be due to the incorrect assumption that either no intervention is needed, or that someone else has already taken action, through calling the police for example. In every case, the simplest and most effective method for countering the bystander effect is to call out the individual and to make them aware of their own inaction and the consequences of it. In other words, to do what you can to increase their self-awareness. The importance of this tendency not to speak up or intervene has obvious consequences within organisations when things go wrong. It is interesting to note that an additional factor influencing people's reluctance to intervene is the extent to which they believe someone more qualified to take action is present. This points to the likely probability that the appointment of experts in culture, risk management or ethics will negatively impact on the likelihood of people speaking out. The bystander effect is another great example of the mechanism through which culture works, assumptions driving behaviours and is a very well-studied area of behavioural psychology. It happens collectively and the effect is stronger when people do not know each other well. This means that it is most likely to be exhibited by newcomers to an organisation or group, or members of teams lacking in cohesion.

The typical reasons why people stay quiet include because they're embarrassed, because they don't want to be wrong or are simply concerned that they could actually make things worse. Perhaps the most plausible reason for inaction is that we don't want to draw attention to ourselves and suffer the possible negative consequences of doing so. Again, a classic example of behaviour memes in action. The decision to act or not is of course made almost immediately. We sum up the situation, make assumptions regarding the potential costs and consequences, and make the decision about how to act all in a split second. You may argue that this fact makes it different from other types of whistleblowing which don't require such an immediate response and are not time critical. But once you've made the decision not to speak up or intervene as a negative situation is unfolding, it can be very difficult to go back, even when you have personally had time to consider the situation more carefully. You may well simply look for further justification as to why not speaking up was a morally acceptable course of action. This tendency will of course be counteracted if instead of being left to grapple with the consequences of your actions or inaction alone, people have a safe and supportive forum for discussing and exploring different options and behavioural choices with their peers.

Groupthink occurs when the desire of group members to maintain cohesion becomes a more important consideration than the quality of decision being made. Psychologist Irving Janis, described groupthink as;

> *"A deterioration of mental efficiency, reality testing, and moral judgment that results from in-group pressures."*

Such pressures could include dominant leadership, intolerance for dissent or an unrealistic belief in the competence or integrity of the group. These pressures can dissuade people from voicing their opinions and when people remain silent, an illusion of agreement or unanimity can quickly be created within the group. This in turn makes the likelihood of other members voicing their disagreement less likely. An important feature of groupthink is that the decisions reached are often more extreme than any single group member would have originally countenanced, resulting in unethical decisions and agreed courses of action.

Irving Janis described the most effective way of counteracting groupthink as to make sure that every team member knows what it is, and how it can influence decisions. A self-aware group that is able to recognise the symptoms of groupthink are naturally far less likely to succumb to its negative effects. Members who are aware of groupthink and able to recognise its impact on them personally are more likely to voice their opinion when it differs from the prevailing norm and to introduce new ideas into the conversation. Innovation and creative problem solving are more likely to thrive in this environment and the quality of decisions will be enhanced. In other words, individual self-awareness is key to avoiding the potential pitfalls of groupthink.

What these very well researched phenomena illustrate is that the range of forces influencing the behaviour of anyone acting within a group are significant, and that the behaviour as a group member is likely to be very different from their behaviour as an individual. In some instances, such as social facilitation, these forces can have a positive impact, but in most others they will be malign. With phenomena such as deindividuation, groupthink and the bystander effect, the impact will always be undesirable, and these forces normally exert their effects in a way that the individual has little or no consciousness of. In each case, the most effective way to combat any negative impact on behaviour is to help people to maintain self-awareness to enable them to act consciously in line with their normal morals and values. This helps individuals understand what behaviours or decisions are unacceptable and to guide them as to when it is appropriate to speak out or act. This has profound implications for how we try to deal with negative consequences of group membership, in that in every case, the most effective means of combatting them resides at the level of the individual rather than the collective. Despite all of what we know about how to counteract the influence of group membership on the individual, almost all of the common culture assessment and change interventions we use have their focus at the level of the group. We tinker with structures and processes, embark on large-scale, high-level change and communications programmes. But our success in defining, describing and remediating group phenomena has in every case been down to our focus on the interface between the individual and the group. In the context of social psychology, it is inconceivable that we would ever look to design interventions that would have their focus anywhere else, yet this is a lesson that we appear to be incapable of applying to the context of organisational culture. Top-down change programmes, mass communications campaigns, surveys and assessments which only present aggregated data at the organisational or subgroup level will ultimately be ineffective if they do not take account of the fundamental need to build self-awareness at the level of the individual.

To return to our avian analogy, is it any wonder that we fail to understand the forces at work within the murmuration when we look at it in its entirety. If we only see the intricate swoops and swirls of a murmuration, then just as the early observers did, we're likely to conclude that the flock is incredibly complex and impossible to predict or manage, or even governed by completely unknown and mysterious forces such as thought transference. And yet when we do look at it from the perspective of the individual and its interaction with its immediate neighbours, we can begin to understand the mechanics of it in simple terms. This is precisely what we need to do with culture and yet we seem unable or reluctant to do so. Why is it inconceivable that something so complex cannot be distilled down to basic rules and processes when we know this is true of every other complex system science has been able to describe?

You will never stop people behaving like unthinking drones by treating them like unthinking drones. If people are excluded from deciding what change is required, they will inevitably be alienated from the entire change process. Time and again during change programmes we hear complaints that people feel excluded, decisions are made behind closed doors and change is being imposed upon them. In response, rather than being actively resistant, people simply opt out, something that ultimately results in the same thing, no change at all. Traditional change models focus on the achievement of an outcome with respect to large groups rather than the creation of the process through which individuals can actively participate. Any effective solution has to take a more people-centred methodological approach which in itself facilitates change. This takes the focus away from the specific outcomes we are looking to affect and puts it on the process through which change itself is the resulting by-product.

The traditional view of change consulting stresses a mechanistic process through which an organisation's culture is assessed, restructured, reengineered and fixed from the outside. The theory is that an external perspective is required in order to objectively diagnose what needs to change and how. This is then done through applying a range of tools and processes available to the change agent.

Project teams are convened, complex change roadmaps drafted, communications campaigns planned, 'toolkits' utilised, and processes and procedures redesigned. It is this kind of approach that has resulted in our well-documented failure to change organisational culture.

Organisations whose primary focus is on tinkering with the structural or procedural levers of change risk losing sight of their people and leaving them behind. Everyone needs to have the capacity to act as a change agent. People need this agency in an environment where leadership and followership are not defined by rigid hierarchical structures, in other words, they need to have the implicit permission to make decisions and take actions without approval. In this scenario, the role of leadership moves from providing control and direction to providing a safe and supportive environment where change can happen.

If we are to accept that large organisations are self-organising entities and that culture emerges from these complex systems, we need to shift our emphasis from the role of the change agent being seen as pulling the levers of change to creating the conditions under which change occurs organically and naturally. The behaviour of people within an organised system cannot be changed through manipulation, coercion or force. Change has to happen because they are personally aware of the need for and benefit of it. In order to do this, people need to be sufficiently aware of their own behaviour, as well as that of others, so that they can consciously make the changes that are needed. The forces for change are neither top down, nor bottom up, they are inside out, with the impetus for change coming from within. This way, the role of the change agent is to remove barriers and help everyone have unfamiliar kinds of conversations, creating new perspectives that lead to new behaviours and assumptions.

We must never underestimate the power of the self-reinforcing mechanisms which characterise organisational cultures. These will inevitably serve to resist change and maintain the status quo. Those who have benefitted most within the current culture may fear losing certainty, along with the power and influence they hold. Past failures in driving change are likely to fuel cynicism and apathy. Changes will inevitably require managers and leaders to let go of established practices, relinquish familiar means of control, and utilise new skills, all of which can be extremely destabilising and even threatening to their authority. The new role of the traditional change agent will also be unfamiliar to both consultants and organisational leadership. Traditional views of leadership and followership will also no longer apply, neither will the old certainties about the role of the external expert.

All these considerations mean that we cannot take a piecemeal approach to assessment, communications and development. We need to deploy an integrated methodology that brings assessment, feedback, support, communications, and skills development together into one coherent whole. We also need a means of monitoring activity to ensure that the right things are happening across what may be a very large organisation. The good news is that the practical tools to help coordinate all these activities are increasingly growing in sophistication. It has often been said that technology alone will never change culture. This is true, but only in as much as nothing has the power to change a culture other than the people within it. What technology can do very effectively however is to help create the conditions under which culture change can happen in a consistent way across even the largest of organisations. Most importantly, technology can do this in a way that is not prohibitively resource intensive.

For many years now, organisations have had access to online tools for a range of different purposes from large-scale surveying and reporting to social media for collaboration and ideation, to training and development platforms. Traditionally these have been used in isolation, with little coordination in terms of timing, physical location, or coherence of purpose. This is against the backdrop that organisations are becoming increasingly diffuse and loose in their structure, a trend that has been hugely accelerated by the pandemic and the increase in remote working, virtual teams and a move away from the traditional office environment. There has never been a greater need or opportunity to bring these functions into one coherent whole using integrated tools specifically designed for the purpose of supporting change. Tools with integrated technical capabilities are already starting to emerge and these can only improve in their scope, sophistication, and flexibility in the near future. The technical capabilities of such systems are clearly not the only determinant of their utility, as much depends upon the extent to which the different content elements are designed in a way that complement one another. This is not a simple task and requires a multi-disciplinary approach involving expertise in assessment design, data analysis and presentation, facilitation, training and communications. But as we have seen, many organisations are currently falling at the very first hurdle.

So, if we want to facilitate an inside out approach to building better organisational cultures, where do we start? The answer has to be where the impacts of group membership are felt most often and most acutely. Everyone from the boardroom down is part of a team, and every team has team regular, scheduled meetings. The behavioural principles which exemplify how effective culture is, or is not, are never more clearly demonstrated than within the context of team interactions. Adherence to the basic best-practices that apply equally to everyone within formalised face to face interactions is the ideal starting point for improvements in less formal settings. The problem is that many interactions fail to provide an exemplification of the desired cultural state. A great place to start is therefore to systematically look to enhance the quality of team interactions through better team meetings.

In many cases even the most basic best practices are not followed. For example, team meetings should at the very least provide a structure for managing daily interactions and provide an equal opportunity for all to participate. Despite this, many meetings do not even have a formal, pre-defined agenda, and therefore no clear structure. Meeting agendas do more than just provide a structure, they enable everyone to prepare to participate. Introverted or deeply analytical co-workers may be inhibited from participating without an opportunity to gather their thoughts in advance. Allowing everyone space to prepare and to then contribute their comments or ideas in turn helps ensure that different perspectives can be heard, especially from those less able or inclined to offer them during the more usual cut and thrust of less structured discussions.

Effective team meetings create a climate where everyone can actively participate, make themselves heard and feel like a valued member of the team. The truth is that for various reasons many team members can feel reluctant to contribute, or when they do, feel that their contributions are not as welcome or valued as they might be. The good news is that if some basic ground rules are consistently followed, team meetings can provide an environment where all team members can actively participate, influence decisions, and feel a strong sense of belonging. The ability to conduct inclusive meetings is a learned skill, and every manager can do it if a few basic ground rules are consistently followed. So, what practical steps can we follow to make out team meetings more inclusive?

The first step is incredibly simple, but rarely taken in practice. This is to agree some non-negotiable ground rules which should govern the functioning of the team. These should consist of basic behaviour-based rules that define what is acceptable and unacceptable. These can be as simple as not interrupting or belittling any contribution and giving everyone an opportunity to participate fully. An important point to make here is that team members themselves should be given the shared responsibility to define what these ground rules should be rather than having them imposed upon them. They should also be required to police these rather than management, who should resist the opportunity to automatically step in and intervene. These steps will obviously increase ownership and accountability over the process. There will usually be a requirement to align the team with pre-defined behavioural standards prescribed by a formal values or change programme. In this case the team members should be given the opportunity to apply these as they best see fit, allowing some leeway, but not enough so that any of the core values are broken.

It is fine to disagree during discussions, but agreement should be reached on how to do so politely and respectfully. Disagreements are natural and will occur, but when conflict arises, it must be resolved with calmness and respect, again in clear behavioural terms as defined by the group. During the meeting, steps should be taken to ensure that all team members have an equal opportunity to participate, feel comfortable contributing and have an equal opportunity to influence decisions and outcomes. Many meetings are dominated by the most confident and extraverted members. If this is the case, those who are less confident or outgoing may feel unable or unwilling to contribute. It should be everyone's responsibility to monitor and track participation, keeping tabs on who is doing the talking and who isn't. If the conversation is dominated by a few individuals, nobody should be afraid to step in and give a warm and polite invitation to quieter team members to contribute or to reinforce that all contributions are valued and that every suggestion is given due consideration and is never dismissed out of hand. In these circumstances, time and space should be given for consideration and reflection. Pauses in the conversation are normal and natural and again will provide those less-confident team members an opportunity to process what's being discussed and to organise their thoughts.

Meeting ground rules will need to be reinforced regularly and revisited whenever it is felt appropriate. There will inevitably be cause to change or add to these over time, so they should never be viewed as set in stone. They will however be required to apply equally to informal interactions outside the context of team meetings, they should in this respect constitute the team's behavioural charter.

Much of what informs this behavioural charter will be relatively clear from the outset. We have spent much time exploring how to create inclusive work cultures where risk is managed effectively, and innovation allowed to flourish as these are the universal characteristics of healthy cultures. How these can be encouraged and reinforced will need to be informed by regular objective assessment as well as the subjective experiences of team members. Once agreed, these behavioural ground rules can be logged onto an online system where it can be regularly reviewed and amended as necessary and accessed by coordinating functions or other teams seeking suggestions or ideas. Activity of the right kind can also be monitored and if necessary, incentivised or even mandated so that opting out is not an option.

No change programme can succeed without an understanding of where an organisation is relative to where it needs to be and of progress towards the desired end state. It will also fail if it does not provide meaningful feedback to individuals and teams about the extent to which they are, or are not, supporting change objectives. This makes an assessment a fundamental element of any culture change programme. The starting point for designing this kind of culture assessment has to be to identify your most pressing business needs and clearly define the behaviours which exemplify the culture best suited to addressing these. This and only this will inform what you need to measure. Your descriptions of required key behaviours should be in clear language which define the in observable terms that everyone can relate to. In the example of the US retail bank who focused on encouraging employees to make greater use of their discretion in decision-making, evidence of the need for this particular change came from outside the organisation itself, from the customers. This is common and to be expected, as an external perspective is usually needed to provide a complete and objective view of the need for culture change. By using a range of internal and external perspectives, a 360-degree view of the organisation can be gained, providing a richer view of priorities for change than would otherwise be the case.

In all but the smallest organisations a large-scale quantitative assessment will be required. This may or may not be integrated with some form of qualitative research. The aims of these two types of assessment should be different, but complementary. In most cases, the qualitative research would be deployed at the very beginning to identify the desired behaviours and the assumptions which act as barriers to their adoption. These insights can then inform the design of a quantitative assessment. In medium to large organisations, this quantitative assessment would typically take the form of a large-scale data collection exercise such as an online survey of employees. In order to allow for reporting down to team levels, and to ensure inclusion of everyone in the process, a census of all employees is usually appropriate. Despite the organisational perspective this approach provides us, we must never lose sight of the individual when reporting on the data collected. Luckily, the most up to date assessment systems have the capability of automatically generating and feeding response data back to individual respondents. This way every participating employee can receive direct feedback regarding their own levels of alignment with cultural change objectives for example, without the violation of any confidentiality requirements. Similarly, the results for teams, divisions or entire organisations can be automatically aggregated and reports distributed according to a pre-defined hierarchy. This provides users at all levels with the data relevant to them in a format that is appropriate to the requirements of the user. Individual reports need to raise each employee's awareness of their own personal understanding and assumptions around the current and desired behaviours, while team reports should aim to facilitate the right kinds of conversations between the team members. Divisional and organisational reports are best presented in the form of interactive online dashboards that allow for the identification of high-level interventions, structural or procedural changes. These can also incorporate data from other sources such as customer feedback and performance metrics so that any relationships between them can be identified. Such dashboards are also invaluable in the identification of local sub-cultures and pockets of best practice.

These powerful platforms for the assessment and reporting of cultural data can be quickly and cost-effectively deployed across even the largest and most complex of organisations. With regular insights, consensus can be reached, progress can be tracked, and best practices can be identified and shared. Many of these platforms have the added bonus of incorporating practical tools to encourage involvement and ideation. For example, individual employees can post their own suggestions for change, respond to the suggestions of others, or share successful approaches across open or closed online peer communities. One of the real benefits of these systems is that all activity can be automatically logged and reported on demand. This makes the task of identifying which individuals and teams are doing the right things, and who are not, much easier. Then, rather than rewarding results in terms of scores that can readily be manipulated, we are now able to track and reward the right kinds of activities that are likely to result in the right kind of outcomes. Those who are complacent, delegating activity to others or simply dragging their feet can be quickly identified and incentivised to play more of an active role.

Another real benefit of these platforms is that they can also support skills development, particularly relating to team and management effectiveness. Developmental materials in a range of formats can be accesses through the same portals as assessment, reporting and collaboration tools. These can include formalised training materials, team discussion guides for managers, snap 'pulse' or guided surveys into specialised topic areas. This helps to bring all these otherwise disparate elements into a single whole, not only in terms of physical location, but notionally as part of a single coherent initiative. Again, active participation can be measured as well as regular ongoing assessment to assess the impact on team culture and individual experience.

16

THE FUTURE OF CULTURAL ASSESSMENT AND MANAGEMENT

Covid 19 has had a profound impact on the way many of us work and the relationship we have with our employers. It has forced an acceleration in many trends that were already underway. The most obvious of these has been the move toward remote working as part of virtual teams. Much will be with us indefinitely and the accelerated move to remote working through virtual teams precipitated by COVID 19 will undoubtedly be to a greater or lesser extent irreversible. On the face of it, this would seem to make the task of creating and reinforcing a desired culture all the more difficult. Remote working would appear to present us with a problem because it removes employees from the direct personal interactions that characterise the culture we may wish to cultivate, to cause a dilution of the forces that create and reinforce culture. This change may however have unexpected benefits in that for any organisation looking to manage its culture against this backdrop, a much more deliberate and structured approach needs to be taken. Organisations will need to be purposeful in terms of how they operationalise culture building through increasingly formalised and indirect interactions. Letting culture drift, or failing to measure it effectively, is even less of an option than it has ever been.

THE FUTURE OF CUTURAL ASSESSMENT AND MANAGEMENT

Another intriguing outcome of the pandemic has been the Great Resignation. During the pandemic, people were plunged into a world which was suddenly highly insecure and unpredictable. When faced with the uncertainties of the pandemic, while at the same time being afforded the time and space to think about their own situation, people increasingly started to look for meaning and purpose in their work and their lives in general. As a result, many employees became much more attuned to the extent to which their basic psychological needs and intrinsic motivators were or were not being satisfied in their work. If they found their work lacking in some important regard, they showed themselves to be more than ready to act decisively and leave their jobs. This process of re-evaluation has resulted in many looking for what it is that creates the greatest meaning and purpose in their lives. Many have clearly concluded that their work as it was, was not high on their list. This increased focus on purpose is likely to prove an example of how the pandemic has speeded up a work trend that was already underway, and one that may also be largely irreversible. Furlough, home working, and reduced hours allowed many to get off the hamster wheel to discover they had plenty of time for reflection and to query some fundamentals of their work lives. The great resignation only happened because in the face of massive environmental change, many people had an opportunity to pause and take stock of what was really important to them.

When discussing the future of culture assessment and management we can't ignore the role of technology. In this, we have to include artificial intelligence, or machine learning and its likely impact. The history of work since the industrial revolution has primarily been a story of people outsourcing much of their work to machines. This primarily involved repetitive physical tasks which were most easily mechanised. We are now at the point where machines appear to be ready to replicate many of our mental as well as physical capabilities so that we can also outsource much of the cognitive work that humans had hitherto undertaken to them. Indeed, in many cases artificial intelligence can already demonstrably outperform humans. AI systems can take in a constant stream of very large amounts of new information and have the capacity to learn and make more and more accurate decisions based on this information. AI systems seem intelligent to us because they unerringly do precisely what they are asked to do and the more data they receive, the better their decision-making. What's more, the quality of this decision making is never negatively impacted by boredom or fatigue. But it is precisely these qualities that make AI particularly suitable to low level, routine cognitive tasks requiring strict adherence to rigid procedure. For time-sensitive tasks involving the rational analysis of large amounts of data, AI is clearly superior to humans. Humans frequently make irrational decisions, particularly when we persist in our existing beliefs despite compelling evidence to the contrary. In many instances we can therefore expect AI-powered systems to overcome this problem through the rigid application of algorithms and logic. In situations that require nuanced decision making involving the use of intuition, empathy and situational sensitivity, humans still have the upper hand. Nevertheless, artificial intelligence still presents people-centric managers and functions with an obvious dilemma. How can we maintain a human approach to people management while at the same time take advantage of the benefits offered by AI?

People management functions are currently most likely to be using AI in the context of talent management, particularly in the areas of recruitment and retention. One of the biggest benefits that AI offers hiring managers is the ability to identify suitable candidates for jobs and can work very well at the start of the recruitment process. This is the most likely application because AI systems can quickly and accurately perform a preliminary analysis of a candidate's résumé to cross-check his/her declared skills or experience against those predefined as job critical. For example, résumés can be screened for all kinds of basic, routine information about work experience or education especially in situations where there are many applicants for a limited number of openings. The task of sifting through a large number of résumés in the traditional way can be very routine and time-consuming, but AI based systems can do it in a fraction of the time it would take humans and with much greater accuracy. They also have the capacity to be fairer in that they deploy a process which is effectively 'blind' to additional information irrelevant to the screening process which has been shown to introduce bias. These include the assumptions human screeners can make regarding a candidate's race, gender or socio-economic background for example.

AI systems are great at performing routine tasks of this kind as well as synthesising large amounts of data, but problems arise when we expect them to be too clever. For example, many systems utilise video interviews and even emotion recognition software in the candidate selection process. Predictive models which attempt to identify suitable candidates based on the profile of existing employees who have been adjudged high performers, or most likely to be successful and loyal are also increasingly being deployed. The problem with these more complex tasks is that AI systems only do what you ask them to. If you ask them to predict who will perform well and progress, or stay with your organisation, they will do it. They will develop algorithms based on current patterns of behaviour and background data to predict future outcomes. When fed current data they will inevitably do it within the strict boundaries of your existing culture. This means that when they are fed performance data which reflects the current biases in processes and systems, these biases will be hard baked into their algorithms. They will identify top performers and loyal employees based on who else has always been successful and loyal within the current cultural context. In this way they may increase conformity, reduce diversity in its broadest sense as well as the size of your organisational meme pool. In this way, AI algorithms can create a self-fulfilling prophesy, a hyper efficient self-reinforcing feedback loop.

As we have seen, successful and loyal employees have inevitably become so within the context of an existing culture. To use the profile of existing employees as a template for an ideal future employee is an extremely efficient way of perpetuating existing biases and ensuring that future change will be even more difficult than it otherwise would have been. There are obviously means that we can deploy to help ensure that we maintain a representative employee population in terms of factors such as race and gender at all levels. But this is much more difficult to do when we are looking to maintain the wider diversity that brings with it the full range of commensurate organisational benefits. For example, in many positions, especially those requiring people management, a candidate's inherent empathy, creativity or self-awareness are worth more than past experience and skills. There can also be a distinct bias against neurodivergent candidates. These are all the kinds of factors that AI is inherently unable to take account of. Nonetheless decreasing the time taken up by repetitive, low-value tasks certainly appears to present us with an opportunity to help people managers dedicate more time to strengthening workplace bonds and developing the relationships that build effective work cultures. Whether or not this will be the result is very much remains to be seen.

The obvious solution to such problems is not to use AI as a proxy for more complex human decision making, but instead to complement and inform it. The insights provided by AI should be used as just another source of data with decision makers still being expected to use their judgement to make the call. This way their understanding about cultural aspirations, about individuals and teams need to be brought to bear as well as human traits of empathy and compassion when reaching a decision. The ability of humans to imagine and anticipate future outcomes, making situational judgements against a background of change, particularly with regard to balancing short and long-term considerations, is unique. Human intelligence can be considered authentic rather than artificial as it allows for effective judgements to be made within the open, constantly changing system of a modern working environment. Rather than looking to subcontract more and more human activities out to machines, it is the organisations who truly embrace this reality that will succeed in future. The potential that AI has to improve productivity through the automation of cognitively routine work offers all kinds of potential benefits. The trick in using it effectively lies in creating the conditions under which a transformational mindset allows AI to be embraced and proactively integrated with existing human capabilities. Only then can we create a whole which is more than the sum of its parts.

Maintaining truly effective future work cultures in the light of advances in AI does not have to mean an inevitable adaptation to mass redundancies and increasing human obsolescence. Lurid predictions regarding the extent to which AI will replace humans in the workplace may well be, at least for the short to medium term, largely unfounded. AI can instead contribute to the creation of working environments where we humans can add the maximum value by doing what they do best. This way they have the capacity to be more efficient, secure and fulfilled in the execution of their jobs, relieved of the responsibility for the most repetitive and unrewarding tasks. Far from creating culturally impoverished and more transactional workplaces, the technological advances AI presents us with open the doors to building healthier, more inclusive, people-centred cultures. Whether this happens or not depends entirely on how we choose to deploy these new tools.

One of the most alarming applications of AI in the attempted control of large numbers of people has been reported from China. The slogan *One Person, One File* has been used to describe how the use of multiple different data sources are being used to track individuals with the aim of predicting their future behaviour using AI. Facial recognition technology, surveillance footage and online activity of all kinds is all gathered on an ongoing basis for this purpose. The pretext for this has been to enable them to better predict crime, but many commentators have been sceptical about the precise motives of the Chinese authorities. This scepticism has been fuelled by the fact that China is reported to be developing and testing a scanning system designed to identify facial features characteristic of minority racial groups such as citizens of Uigur descent. Attempts have also been made by police forces in the UK and US to use AI systems to predict where and when crime is likely to happen, with varied success, although they have stopped well short of using it for the purposes of racial profiling.

AI is increasingly impacting on society in a multiplicity of ways and it's just not feasible for this not to play an increasing role in how employers manage their employees in future. In fact, the slogan *One person one file* could easily be applied to employers' HR information systems which hold data of all kinds on every single employee. Organisations are gathering more and more information on employees and increasingly looking for patterns within the data that they have in an attempt to predict a range of behavioural outcomes. Artificial Intelligence is increasingly being deployed to help make sense of all this data. Of course, there is nothing inherently good or bad about this process, again, it's the use to which all this data is put that makes the difference as well as the extent to which we take account of its shortcomings.

Consider the situation of two employees. One works in HR, a function where 70% of employees are female and there is little difficulty recruiting into roles. For the first time in her career, she has been marked *meeting expectations* in her annual performance appraisal. This objective assessment from her new boss, was the lowest she had received in her career, despite the fact that her level of motivation has not changed. She loves her job and doesn't want to leave, but due to a project overrun her workload has increased in recent weeks, and she feels under pressure. She feels less positive about her work than she did previously but knows this is only a temporary situation which will improve as soon as the project comes to an end and things settle down. The other employee works in engineering, an area dominated by male employees and where historically posts have proved hard to fill. She has always been rated as *meeting expectations* in her appraisals and has been keen to leave for some time. She has even started to question whether a career in engineering is right for her. An algorithm identifies them both as a potential flight risk, but the response is very different.

The ensuing conversations with their respective managers are very distinct in content and tone. In the case of the engineer, because of her role, she has been identified as a high priority retention target. The conversation focuses on her developmental path and how her aspirations for progression can be accommodated. She subsequently receives a series of nudges, including notices of internal roles arriving in her email inbox for which she is encouraged to apply for by more senior colleagues. She is also invited to join the account team of an exciting new client. In the case of the HR employee, she is not considered to be such a high priority retention target and the conversation focuses on her drop in performance and a defence of the performance management process that led her to be rated as average. For the first time in her career, she is now considering whether this is the place for her after all.

Of course, ensuring that there is a healthy level of diversity within all job functions, especially in STEM roles, is a very important consideration. But the problem here is that individual situations, motivations and preferences has been completely subsumed by high-level organisational priorities. The machinations of the AI system have been allowed to result in a somewhat less than people-centred outcome. While performance and behaviours were tracked and processed, the AI systems proved to be unable to attribute causation. A drop in performance is often considered a sign of disengagement and an intention to leave, but it can equally well be due to factors such as burnout. In the case of the employee from HR, it was likely that her drop in performance was due to a temporary overload rather than a more permanent change in her attitude with regard to her employer. Any dissatisfaction expressed a change in her transient sentiment rather than a deeper seated and more lasting change in her level of engagement. The AI algorithms were unable to make this important distinction. In other words, they were incapable of understanding why each employee behaved the way they did. They are also incapable of articulating why they come to the decisions they do, beyond providing a simple rules based score. It should have been incumbent on human judgement to take account of these shortcomings in the ensuing face to face discussion. Instead, what is often provided is an attempted justification for the algorithm-based decision.

The recent French IKEA snooping scandal provides us a worrying glimpse of one possible future regarding organisational culture and it is interesting to see the role HR played in the process. A group of employees from Human Resources was accused of working with private investigator and police officers to trawling through employees' data to investigate aspects related to their finances and personal lives. Ikea admitted to infringing on its employees' privacy but denied that this had constituted what was referred to as '*a widespread system of espionage*'. One of the key questions here is whether incidents such as this presage HR's move from a support function to something more akin to a data gathering and monitoring function. Again, this raises questions about the potential for what is supposed to be the corporate function primarily responsible for taking a people centred approach.

AI powered tools designed to monitor communications across large organisations are already emerging. These can integrate with a range of channels such as email, Slack or Microsoft Teams to gather and analyse huge amounts of data. These systems deploy natural language processing and are 'trained' to define the subject of, and sentiment expressed in each interaction according to a detailed coding framework. They effectively track, categorise and quantify all electronic communications between employees. These tools are marketed as helping with

THE FUTURE OF CUTURAL ASSESSMENT AND MANAGEMENT

the early identification of issues such as turnover risk, burnout and engagement levels, so that early remedial interventions can be deployed. These are indeed very important areas to understand and address proactively, and vendors are keen to draw attention to the built-in mechanisms to protect individual anonymity and confidentiality, but none the less, the potential for misuse these kinds of tools is obvious.

17

CONCLUSIONS

There is no downside to getting culture right. Organisations, employees, customers and wider society will all benefit in future if we do. What we need to do is focus on providing an environment where people feel a sense of belonging and valued for the unique perspective and talents they can bring, while their intrinsic motivational factors are provided for. These are not incidental or nice to haves and in no way issues of legal compliance and reputation management. You cannot have a healthy functioning culture without them. This doesn't mean helping people fit in to your organisation. It means fitting the organisation around individuals, in all their wonderful variety. We need to consciously let go of traditional mindsets around management and leadership based on power, authority, and control. In future we must rethink what we value in leadership to create a profile that rebalances the desired traits and competencies. Stereotypical mindsets are incredibly resilient, and we cannot simply expect these to change without directly challenging them. This will inevitably be disruptive to many, so the process needs to be supported with the development of alternative behaviours indicative of transformational leadership.

CONCLUSIONS

Nothing is more important than core values, which should never be subsumed by business imperatives, short-term strategy or immediate demands of leadership. Encouraging self-criticality in our ability to live up to them, while balancing the need for people to use their discretion in how we live core values will allow us to build healthy cultures. Raising cultural self-awareness means taking regular time out to talk about how values are or aren't being reflected in our actions. Then everyone can agree a way forward that allows values to be applied in a way that is meaningful and appropriate for each group or team. Giving team members the agency to police formalised behavioural charters based around core values will build accountability and trust. Never make the mistake of assuming that the task of inculcating group values is a purely communications or training challenge. It is in large part a behavioural challenge. Even a universally shared consensus about the need for change will not be a driver of change unless we challenge the core assumptions which have created the current status quo. The greatest impetus for change will, by definition, come for the least expected places, from newcomers, younger employees, the quiet voices. Your most experienced people, and those who have succeeded within the current culture, will likely be those least capable of objectivity and will potentially be the biggest barriers to change.

In future, ongoing measurement must always be part of the solution, but we simply must do it properly. We cannot automatically believe what people tell us, no matter how reassuring it may be. Instead, we need to believe what they do and take steps to identify why they are doing it. Any measurement which does not directly provide information that raises individual awareness is a wasted opportunity. Measurement, analysis and feedback tools can now easily be Integrated with development, communications, and monitoring systems but while technology can help to create the conditions for change, we must always maintain a people-centred perspective.

COUNTING THE DANCE STEPS

We need to ditch the demonstrably false belief that cultures can somehow be fixed from outside or even from inside through expert and specialist team led initiatives. People are fundamentally not resistant to change, they simply don't think it applies to them. People will continue to see culture as somebody else's problem and something that's done to them unless we move away from a traditional view of the change agent and recognise everyone's role in creating and reinforcing change. It's imperative to do everything we can to make change everyone's responsibility, to give them agency and hold them to account. This means moving our focus away from imposing change, to creating the conditions within which change can happen. We cannot continue making the mistake of believing that communication plans, change management initiatives, change management models will make any difference either directly or indirectly. Changing procedures and processes can only reinforce culture change that has already happened, not create it. These are artifacts that will have no impact without real behavioural change to support them.

If we are ever to get to a place where we are managing risk effectively, we have to accept that everyone has the capacity for wrongdoing and any response that does not enhance learning is a wasted opportunity. This will allow us to be honest about and less intolerant of behavioural lapses, but more considered and balanced when we impose sanction for transgression. Admitting to mistakes and individual and collective shortcomings is not a sign of weakness, it is quite the reverse. Relax the reins of control while helping people become more aware of what drives their behaviour and maintaining constant vigilance. Only this will result in an environment where inevitable errors or transgressions have the minimum possible negative consequences.

All this means challenging all the existing received wisdom about culture, its measurement and management. Let's finish by rewriting the current narrative.

CONCLUSIONS

Your culture can be your competitive advantage. Get it right and there are untold benefits. Get it wrong and it could destroy you. While complex, it is not complicated, as it consists of simple building blocks which can be understood and changed in a targeted way. We know how culture works and what it's for. The route to changing culture is not through the use of academic models, expensive specialist consultants or the application of elaborate change or communications programmes. The key to success lies in building cultural self-awareness and creating the conditions under which change can happen while allowing everyone to become a part of the solution. Culture consists of shared assumptions driving collective behaviours and as such can be measured, quantified, and tracked, if only we apply the right tools to enable us to do so. We know precisely what elements contribute to a healthy culture and we can define what a 'good' culture looks like. This allows us to identify what practices should be shared and replicated within and between organisations and sectors. Culture change cannot be a one-off project, but a continuous endeavour and under the right conditions, change can happen relatively quickly without the need for enormous expenditure of money or resources. If we succeed in this endeavour, there will be no losers. Organisations, their employees, customers and wider society will all reap the rewards. It is positively negligent to continue letting our organisational cultures drift unmanaged. To continue to do so is the road to ruin.

Printed in Great Britain
by Amazon

350547b6-25f5-4108-acb9-1ba49b82a47dR01